INNOVATION NAVIGATION

How to get from Idea to Reality in 90 Days

Written by Kurt Baumberger

Co-Created by global Executives, Marketers,
Entrepreneurs, Consultants, and Agencies

Designed by Annika Kappenstein
Illustrated by Holly Fisher

Second Edition

MarketSquare Worldwide
Atlanta, GA, USA
Copyright © 2014 – 2016 Kurt Baumberger
All rights reserved

Library of Congress Cataloging-in-Publishing Data

Baumberger, Kurt
Innovation Navigation: How To Get From Idea To Reality In 90 Days
ISBN: 978-0-9908964-1-8

Book Design by Annika Kappenstein, Amala Design Group (http://amaladesign.com)
Illustrations by Holly Fisher (http://spence-creative.com)

References to website URLs were accurate at the time of printing. Neither the author nor MarketSquare Worldwide is responsible for URLs that may have expired or changed since the manuscript was prepared.

To Katie & Griffin

A child is the ultimate innovation. You both make me very proud.

in · no ·

va·tion

noun

1: the introduction of something
   substantially and meaningfully new
2: a radically new idea, method, or device

Synonyms: brainchild, breakthrough,
creation, invention, transformation

Antonyms: copy, clone, duplicate,
imitation, replication, reproduction

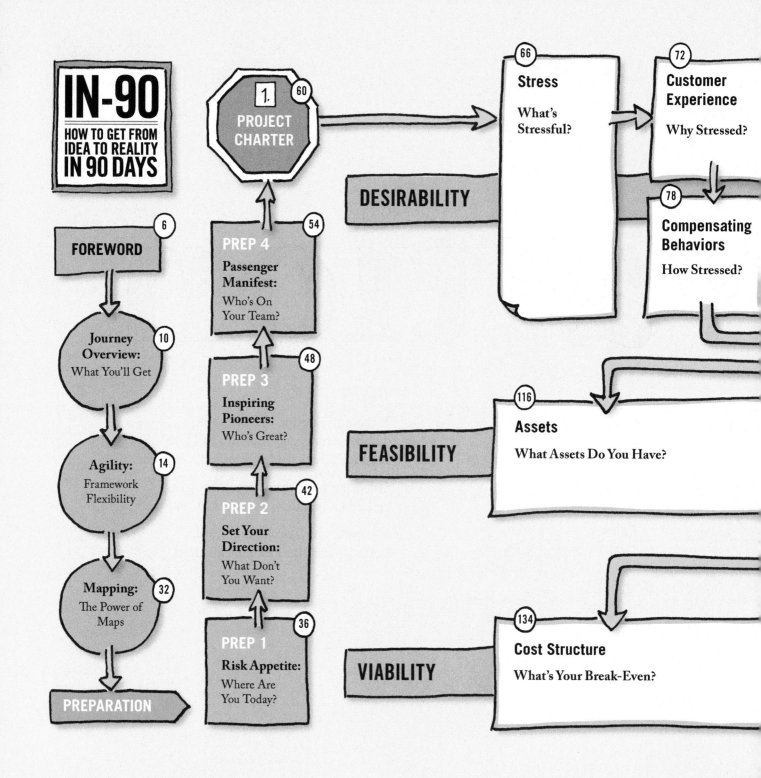

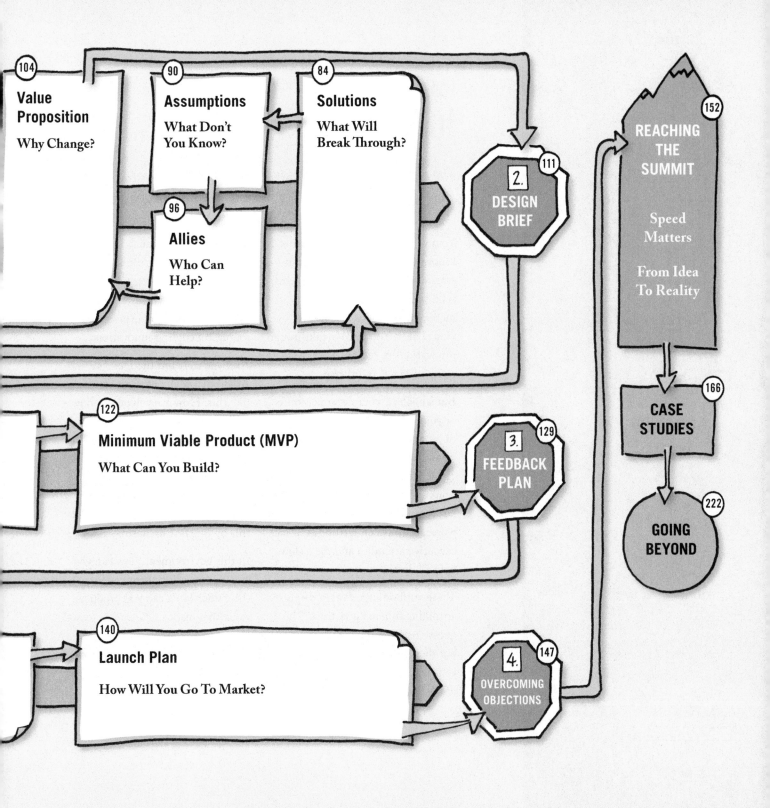

HERE'S THE CHALLENGE

They always say time changes things, but you actually have to change them yourself. — *Andy Warhol, Artist*

Your organization desperately needs innovation to create new revenue streams or solve complex problems. And you know that small incremental improvements just won't cut it. You need breakthrough innovations to remain competitive—and thrive.

But somehow your organization or your client's organization is full of "antibodies" that seem to kill innovations before they ever have a chance to germinate and grow. You've pitched many "Big Ideas," but they don't go anywhere. Or worse, they are underfunded or lack executive attention and die a slow, painful death.

These antibodies are often disguised as mild mannered questions. The questions seem innocent enough, but they are designed to stop you in your tracks. In his book, *Ten Faces of Innovation*, Tom Kelley from the innovation consultancy IDEO calls this process "facing the Devil's Advocate." According to Kelley, the Devil's Advocate assumes the most negative possible perspective to quash fledgling innovations.

And you've heard the Devil's Advocate speak before. It sounds like this: How are you going to get (insert name here) to agree to this? Who's actually going to do this work? You know your assumptions are way too aggressive, don't you? Where are you going to get the funding for this? Have you passed this by Legal, Purchasing, and IT?

In this environment, how can you create innovation that changes the game? How can you produce value that inspires customers to act? How can you prove your idea has merit to those people seemingly bent on destroying anything that is new, different, and special?

It's admittedly not easy. You're stretched to capacity, spend your time rushing from meeting to meeting, just trying to process the tasks coming your way. How many times have you sat in a meeting and worked on your email, texts, or presentations just to make sure you don't drop the ball on something else?

Where does all this pressure to execute tasks (and kill innovation) come from? Well, it's pretty simple. The focus of any established organization, and especially large organizations, is to make sure the organization operates efficiently in a highly predictable and quantifiable way.

Because these organizations have an insatiable desire for control, they use incremental improvement methodologies such as Lean Six Sigma or ISO 9001 or a Stage-Gate decision making process, and unconsciously quash breakthrough innovation. Over time, these operating environments produce managers who learn to be wary of their own judgment, intuition, and instinct.

Managers end up falling in love with reassuringly familiar numbers from predictable sources where contradictory data can be weeded

out and ignored. They learn to fear entering a meeting with any innovation that challenges the status quo or existing budgets unless they are armed to the teeth with some kind of "proof" that their innovation will work.

But here's the challenge: If there's already proof, then what you're doing is not innovation. If you are measuring success by improving efficiency five percent or reducing some nominal number of man-hours, then don't mislabel your efforts as innovation.

Innovations are inherently journeys into the unknown. Innovations require taking paths not yet charted. Innovations involve risk. Innovations require flexibility and openness to change your direction, e.g., viewpoint, resources, organization structure, to get where you want to go.

For managers who like to wrap themselves in the security of numbers, navigating through the innovation landscape will be frightful. Ironically, the more formal business education you have like an MBA (which I earned at Duke University), the more you are trained seek the security of numbers and avoid the hazards of uncertainty and unpredictability.

But these are the core characteristics of innovation. So it's not surprising that some of the greatest innovators in recent memory like Bill Gates, Steve Jobs, and Mark Zuckerberg never even graduated from college.

Fortunately, there's hope — you're holding it in your hands. You see, over a lifetime of launching (and failing to launch) breakthrough innovations from Advil and *USA TODAY* to mobile phone applications and electric cars, I've learned there's only one thing that works — a time-tested, battle-hardened regimen designed to accelerate ideas to reality in 90 days.

This regimen is called IN-90.™ The IN-90 regimen requires a high level of intensity for ninety consecutive days. It uses a structured innovation framework and Agile Methodology, combined with rapid prototyping and customer feedback.

During the program, you will complete maps that identify customer stresses, causes of stress, compensating behaviors and emotion levels, allies, value propositions, assets, minimum viable product (MVP) functionality, break-even, and a launch plan. Underlying this mapping process is an Agile Methodology requiring 15-minute daily scrums and bi-weekly executive feedback sessions.

The IN-90 regimen relies on building rapid prototypes. These prototypes can be simple, unsophisticated models as long as they can be taken into the marketplace to gain additional learning from customers. The insights from customers serve as catalysts to produce the next prototype and this iterative process continues until the innovation team agrees there are diminishing returns on building another prototype.

Here's why you need IN-90: Ninety percent of all innovation projects die after their ninetieth day of life. *Harvard Business Review* reported in "Why Good Projects Fail Anyway" and "Why Big Companies Can't Innovate" that innovation projects lasting longer than ninety days fail for one of three reasons: entrenched processes, unexpected changes (e.g., management, funding priorities, innovation team), or unmanageable scope. As a good steward of your organization who understands these dynamics, you can't afford not to adopt the IN-90 regimen.

There are thousands of innovation books available today. But there's only one guide that combines a proven framework, Agile Methodology, rapid prototyping, and customer feedback to get your idea to reality in ninety days. This guide is packed full of lessons I've learned working with creative geniuses like Ken Burns and Jay Chiat, great leaders like Colin Powell and Mike Krzyzewski, and legendary entrepreneurs like Steve Jobs and Dave Thomas.

This guide also contains the highlights from over 200 books on innovation. If you've ever wanted a distilled version of the insights from Peter Drucker, Malcolm Gladwell, Seth Godin, Chip and Dan Heath, Guy Kawasaki, and Tom and David Kelley, then look no further.

And if there's one thing that all of these minds believe is that innovation is about building something. It's about having a bias for action. It's about getting out into the world with a tangible physical representation of your idea.

Why? Because until you get out and talk deeply with customers, you won't know where they find value. You won't know what's important and why. You're likely to face unexpected findings, uncertainty, and people who say things you don't want to hear.

But the payoff is grand. Because it's in the marketplace that you will find keen insights and make creative breakthroughs. Going out in search of learning opens you up to new information and ideas that will never come to you if you don't leave your office.

More important, your credibility skyrockets within your organization when you can say, "I've seen what people do. I've observed our customers in their environment. I know what they really need, and it's not what we thought."

Fortunately, you don't need a multi-million dollar investment to create breakthrough innovations. You just need to commit to an intense ninety day effort and lean on a proven regimen. Each step of the journey you'll build your confidence and the confidence of others as you get from idea to reality in ninety days!

Best wishes,

Go see what people do. Observe your customers in their own environment. Then you'll know what they really need... AND IT'S PROBABLY NOT WHAT YOU THINK...

WHAT YOU'LL GET

Everything should be as simple as possible, but not simpler.
— *Albert Einstein, Physicist*

Einstein not only solved mysteries of the universe, but he also recognized that the starting point for any good discussion, meeting, or collaboration should be a shared understanding of what is being considered.

This guide is for you if you are constantly thinking about how to improve your organization, or if you are trying to find innovative ways to grow your business, or if you are in business development trying to sell your BIG IDEA to new or existing customers.

Most of the time, you'll hold a job role as a:

- ► Senior Executive
- ► Marketer
- ► Product Developer
- ► Salesperson
- ► Consultant
- ► Agency Executive

These types of people are responsible for innovation in some way or another. But they all need a new approach because the old ways aren't working. They want to be change agents, not efficiency engineers.

Here's What You'll Get

If you follow the IN-90 regimen, here's what you'll get:

1. **The 90-Day Innovation Navigation Framework**
Similar to the popular Business Model Canvas and Lean Startup Methodology, you need a simple innovation framework that everyone understands — one that facilitates description and discussion. It must be clear, relevant, and intuitively understandable, while not oversimplifying the complexities of how organizations truly function.

The framework addresses the only innovation questions that matter:

What's Desirable?
What's needed or wanted badly enough to separate customers from their hard-earned cash or precious time?

What's Feasible?
What can your organization build that's significantly cheaper, better, faster, or more convenient?

What's Viable?
What can your organization deliver, support, and grow that will generate sufficient profits or growth for your shareholders, investors, or owners?

It's at the intersection of these three questions that breakthrough innovations occur.

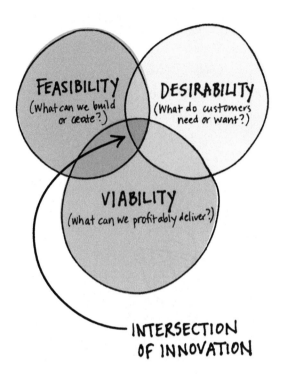

FEASIBILITY
(What can we build or create?)

DESIRABILITY
(What do customers need or want?)

VIABILITY
(what can we profitably deliver?)

INTERSECTION OF INNOVATION

The regimen forces you to ask a lot of questions, but it doesn't allow for cookie-cutter answers because your innovation challenge is unique to you.

2. Time-tested, Battle-hardened Regimen

It's tough enough to innovate. People responsible for innovation need to know that this regimen works. This process has been used by Google, Apple, Nissan, Tesla, The Coca-Cola Company, Hospital Corporation of America, and GE—just to name a few.

This regimen is not theoretical. It's practical. You'll learn about innovation maps—to help you identify what's important, drive decisions, and map your actions so you can launch your innovation. The regimen forces you to ask a lot of questions, but it doesn't allow for cookie-cutter answers because your innovation challenge is unique to you.

3. Tangible Deliverables

Every large organization thrives on documentation because institutional memory is so short (and often wrong.) Here are the maps and documents you'll get:

- ► PREP MAP 1: Where Are You Today?
- ► PREP MAP 2: What Don't You Want?
- ► PREP MAP 3: Who's Great?
- ► PREP MAP 4: Who's On Your Team?
- ► MILESTONE 1: **Project Charter**
- ► MAP 1: What's Stressful?
- ► MAP 2: Why Stressed?
- ► MAP 3: How Stressed?
- ► MAP 4: What Will Break Through?
- ► MAP 5: What Don't You Know?
- ► MAP 6: Who Can Help?
- ► MAP 7: Why Change?
- ► MILESTONE 2: **Design Brief**
- ► MAP 8: What Assets Do You Have?
- ► MAP 9: What Can You Build?
- ► MILESTONE 3: **Feedback Plan**

4. Speed

Finally, adopting the Agile Methodology is essential to accelerate from idea to reality in 90 days. You'll learn how to coordinate and collaborate in fewer than 15 minutes each day. You'll get an imbedded cadence to produce "quick wins" every two weeks. You'll understand how to build a "shippable product" that will build increased confidence in your innovation, your team, and your personal abilities.

Adopting this methodology requires discipline and sacrifice. There will be times when you will have scheduling conflicts, but you need to participate in every call or meeting. Innovation is a contact sport. You cannot be part of the team if you do not practice with the team.

THE FIRST CHANGE IS YOU.

If you want to change the world or, at least, your corner of it, then the first change has to come from you. You'll need to open up your mind to a new approach. You will probably feel uncomfortable at first. You'll be working faster and more collaboratively than you probably have before. You'll need to trust the regimen.

You will be treading in unchartered territory. But others have ventured before you so you might as well learn from their insights, trials, and tribulations. To encourage you, I've listed a quote before each chapter from a fellow trailblazer.

Some quotes are from geniuses like Leonardo da Vinci, Aristotle, and Archimedes. Some quotes are from popular icons like Bob Dylan and The Rolling Stones. Other quotes are from extraordinary inventors like Orville Wright and Albert Einstein.

Let these quotes inspire you. Use them to motivate you. Lean on them to overcome resistance. Remember, it's okay to step on the shoulders of giants. It's how you scale new heights.

GETTING YOUR BEARINGS

When you see the term "reality" used, it refers to a prototype suitable for feedback and input. Even manufacturing companies can create 3-D printing models in 90 days.

Pharmaceutical companies may not be able to produce a drug in 90 days, but they can produce a placebo prototype complete with a name, description, packaging, recommended dosage, and warnings.

Don't worry if your business needs to get government approval before delivering a commercial product or service, you can still build enough functionality to get the feedback you need to reach a "Go/No Go" decision.

FRAMEWORK FLEXIBILITY

Give me a lever long enough and fulcrum on which to place it, and I shall move the world. — Archimedes, Inventor

Because your goal is to propel your organization forward in a key market, or within a critical customer segment, or within a vital distribution channel, you need to develop a breakthrough innovation and not just an incremental improvement. In the past, you've probably jumped quickly into idea generation to see if anything interesting pops out.

In fact, many managers have been taught that the first step in solving a tricky or complex problem is to gather smart people and just start brainstorming. But then you'd be guilty of thinking about the complexity of innovation as a nail just because you know how to swing a hammer. You must first understand *how* to innovate before you *can* innovate.

In this section, I'm going to explain the IN-90 Framework and how it can be flexed five different ways. I'm going to discuss the power of maps and explain why you'll be using maps to complete the framework. Finally, I'll suggest three tips to get the most out of your maps that will make it easier for you to succeed.

The Essence of the IN-90 Framework

Over the years, I've asked thousands of people at hundreds of different organizations to describe what innovation means. Intuitively, they know there are multiple aspects of innovation, but they rarely have the vocabulary to describe the milestones of innovation or how these milestones should guide your innovation journey.

This framework is designed to carefully describe each of these milestones of innovation and clarify what you need to do to

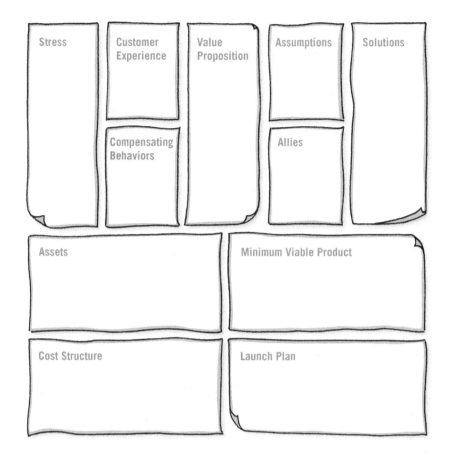

Stress	Customer Experience	Value Proposition	Assumptions	Solutions
Compensating Behaviors		Allies
Assets	Minimum Viable Product
Cost Structure	Launch Plan

This framework will allow you to capture all of the critical components of your innovation on a single page.

implement and commercialize your innovation. But perhaps most important, the framework lets you describe, aggregate, and communicate the rationale of how your organization will create, prototype, and test your innovation on a single piece of paper.

Transforming the historically complex and mysterious art of innovation to something simple and straightforward helps organizations understand the value of your idea while inoculating you from your organization's innovation killing "antibodies." I use the term antibodies metaphorically because organizational objections are just like human antibodies that identify and neutralize foreign objects. Organizational antibodies do the same thing to innovation because it is a foreign object to the status quo.

What Are the Maps?

Let's start with a depiction of the IN-90 Framework and some definitions that will describe and organize how your organization will create, deliver, and capture value to both internal and external customers.

Stresses. What's stressing your customers? How are these stresses impacting behaviors? Emotions? What do these stresses tell you?

Customer Experience. Why are these stresses occurring? What's going on? What's breaking down?

Compensating Behaviors. How bad is the stress? What are customers doing to alleviate their stress?

Solutions. What first-hand insights do you have to help you solve the problem? How can you marry insights with ideas and action?

Assumptions. What critical things do you need to test? What do you want your allies to validate for you?

Allies. Who do you need as your first customers of your innovation? Who else do you need, e.g., distributors, retailers, technology partners? How will they help you speed innovation adoption?

Value Proposition. What will motivate your customers to willingly change to your solution? Is your solution compelling enough for them to come to you with their wallets open?

Assets. What strengths do you have today? What capabilities can you leverage? What else do you need? What do you need to try that you've never tried before?

Minimum Viable Product. What core functionality do you need to test your assumptions? What experiences do you need to create?

Cost Structure. What are customers willing to pay for? How does your innovation impact your current operations? What needs to change? At what cost?

Launch Plan. Who are you targeting? How will you reach them? What will compel them to change their behavior? Why will they believe you?

Stress

What's stressful?

Customer Experience

Why stressed?

Compensating Behaviors

How stressed?

Value Proposition

Why change?

Assumptions

What don't you know?

Allies

Who can help?

Solutions

What will break through?

Assets

What assets do you have?

Minimum Viable Product

What can you build?

Cost Structure

What's your break-even?

Launch Plan

How will you go to market?

The Flexibility of the IN-90 Framework

While the IN-90 Framework might appear to be a simple way to arrange the work that any innovation requires, it is much, much more. Here are five ways you can flex the framework to work for you.

1. Divide the framework into three sections

The IN-90 Framework splits the innovation journey into three stages. The first is the Desirability stage. The second is the Feasibility stage. The third is the Viability stage.

The framework is consciously designed to break out the three core components of innovation: Desirability, Feasibility, and Viability.

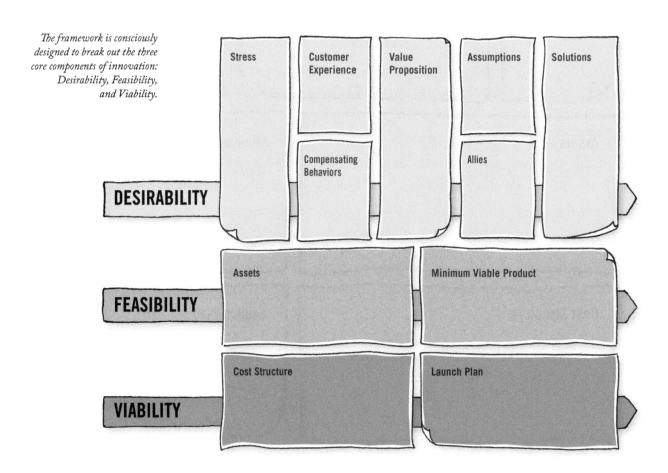

Desirability

Finding out what's desirable starts with understanding the human pain and stresses that customers are experiencing. It's important to note that this pain and stress must be great enough to compel people to willingly change their behavior. They must believe there is a way to alleviate their pain and stress that is better, faster, or cheaper than what they are doing today.

With this deep, human-centric understanding, you can begin to envision a solution that will provide real pain relief or meet a deep need. Your solution will provide the reason why customers select your organization, pay for your product or service, adopt your innovation, or all of the above.

This stage of the innovation journey is often considered the most difficult, but it need not be. Most organizations already have some ideas or insights that just need a regimen to turn them into reality.

Finally, you can articulate why people should change their behavior. You'll be able to explain the new experience you've created and how you've enabled this experience. You can clearly demonstrate what stresses will be alleviated and how your innovation will bring about a new attitude, behavior, or result.

Feasibility

The next stage is about building prototypes of your idea. Building something requires you to take an inventory of the assets you have at your disposal. These assets might be people, processes, technology, or even time and money (although there's rarely ever enough time or money).

As you take this inventory, you'll see not only what you have, but also what you lack. These gaps won't doom you to failure. Instead, they'll help you understand the dangers you're facing so you can either navigate around them or find a way to overcome them.

Once you've collected all of your assets, it's time to build your Minimum Viable Product (MVP). This will be an iterative process very similar to building a house. You may start with a great architectural plan, but hundreds of decisions will have to be made as

Customers must believe your solution is ten times better, faster, or cheaper than what they are doing today.

Let your customers show you where they find real value and they may even pay more!

you build your dream home. The same is true with your innovation—you may have to change course several times before you are able to break through.

Some of my manufacturing clients have questioned whether it's possible to produce an industrial product in such a short time. But with 3-D printing and advanced modeling techniques anything is possible. Remember: You're not building a finished product— just a functional prototype.

Viability

This is often the most exciting stage of the journey. You get to take your innovation to market and find out what's wrong with it. That's right—you focus on what's wrong with it, not what's right with it. Because your customers will show you how well you've addressed their stresses. Collaboration is the goal, not validation of how smart you are.

Let your customers show you where they find value, because it's often not where you think it is. They know their jobs far better than you ever could. So you may think a feature provides a secondary or tertiary benefit when it might be the number one reason for customers to change their behaviors and come running to you eager to buy.

For example, one company I worked with developed a tablet software application for patients to become better educated while in their doctor's waiting room. The company thought this would be a great value to patients since they would be better educated about their condition and doctors would benefit from more informed patients.

But the doctors really didn't care about educating patients. What they really loved was the ability to collect patient ratings and reviews of their practice immediately after the visit that boosted their online reputation. The company discovered that ego-driven doctors were stressed by bad online reviews and were looking for an easy way to counteract negative ratings. Most important for the company, the doctors were willing to pay three times more for a less complicated (and less costly to maintain) application!

So you need to see *how* you're creating value. Keep in mind that innovation is an iterative process. As this example illustrates, you may get all the way to the Viability stage and find an insight that takes you right back to a new set of stresses.

That's okay. In fact, that's great because it means that you have discovered a hidden truth. And if you've discovered it, then it's unlikely your competitors know it and you're better equipped to exploit your advantage.

DON'T TAKE SHORTCUTS

Organizations often want to rush to the Cost Structure map in order to build a financial model. They want to evaluate how much a solution will cost and how much profit will result. DON'T DO THIS.

Here's why. It's an exercise in guesswork. Until you know what assets you have and what you need to build, you won't be able to determine your costs. More important, until you validate your MVP in the market, you'll never know how much you can charge.

But if you can't help yourself and have to do the math, just be sure to list all of your assumptions and estimates on the Assumptions map. This will force you to validate or refute your guesswork.

2. Divide the framework into two hemispheres

The IN-90 Framework also splits the innovation journey into two distinct hemispheres. The left side of the framework focuses on the efficiency side of innovation—operations, productivity, and profit. The right side of the framework focuses on the value of innovation—alleviating stresses, making emotional connections, and overcoming resistance.

Most organizations are quite adept at completing the left side of the framework. That's because large organizations hire, train, and reward people for enhancing and optimizing productivity.

Organizations typically struggle with the right side of the framework. According to an article "Understanding The Services Revolution" by Travis Fagan at McKinsey & Company, "The most successful large companies find a way to force them out of their comfort zone. Walmart is a very interesting example. They took the step of building lab facilities in Silicon Valley for their online platform. They knew they could never make up ground operating out of Bentonville, Arkansas."

So Walmart hired a group of small marketing, technology, and innovation agencies to help them do what they weren't set up to do. Walmart recognized that they are a great commercial logistics company, but they knew they needed smaller firms full of "out of the box" thinkers, designers, and architects to build a customer-centric online experience.

When individuals feel their role is bounded, this allows them to do a significant portion of their work independently, and they are less likely to waste energy negotiating roles or protecting turf.

3. Break up roles and responsibilities map by map

Regardless of whether you're going to build your innovation team with internal people or a combination of internal and external people, you need to ensure you've got clearly defined roles and responsibilities.

It's commonly assumed by innovation team leaders that their most important job is to carefully define the innovation goals and general approach. They believe if they leave the roles of individuals within the team open and flexible, then people will be encouraged to share ideas and contribute in multiple dimensions.

But an article, "Build A Better Innovation Team," published in *Harvard Business Review* reports that behavioral scientists have found the opposite is true: collaboration improves when the roles of individual team members are clearly defined and understood. In fact, when individuals feel their role is bounded, this allows them to do a significant portion of their work independently, and they are less likely to waste energy negotiating roles or protecting turf.

This means you should build an innovation team of specialists, each with their own set of skills to contribute to the innovation team's success. However, each team member should not limit their contribution to their specialty area, but also bring a fresh perspective to work outside their specialty area. This will force a mindset shift from "doing my job" to "doing *the* job."

Efficiency Roles

Product Owner. Brings learning and insights by observing human behavior and understanding how people interact physically and emotionally with products and services

Customer Service Representative. Brings rich stories of people's stresses and what's triggering their stress

Sales Manager or Operations Manager. Brings "front-line" observations of how people compensate for their stresses

Innovation Team Leader. Brings experience in overcoming organization roadblocks to enable the innovation team to strive for breakthrough innovations, not incremental improvements

Finance Manager. Brings experience understanding the financial hurdles and performance thresholds the innovation must meet

Value Roles

Business Solutions Architect. Brings experience from other industries and companies translating those insights to address your unique needs

Project Manager. Brings communication and documentation abilities to track outstanding issues and resolutions

Customer Experience (CX) Architect. Brings design expertise to create compelling experiences that go beyond mere functionality to connect at a deeper level with customer needs

Storyteller. Brings the ability to build organization and customer awareness through compelling narratives that motivate people to act

Prototype Experimenter. Brings the technical skills to rapidly prototype new ideas

Marketing Manager. Brings experience working with cross-functional groups to successfully launch innovations

DEFINE ROLES CLEARLY

Maggie Neal, Director of Managing Teams for Innovation and Success at Stanford University, writes that teams with clearly defined roles and responsibilities are likely to invest more time and energy in a group project because individuals feel that they have "control" over their specialty area, and have the freedom to "edit" the other team members' contributions. This makes each team member feel as though they are intimately involved in all aspects of the innovation while protecting their most precious asset, i.e., their time.

Stress

Product Owner

Customer Experience

Customer Service Representative

Compensating Behaviors

Sales or Operations Manager

Value Proposition

Storyteller

Assumptions

Project Manager

Allies

Customer Experience Architect

Solutions

Business Solutions Architect

Assets

Innovation Team Leader

Minimum Viable Product

Prototype Experimenter

Cost Structure

Finance Manager

Launch Plan

Marketing Manager

The framework clearly defines roles up front so you can demonstrate your respect for everyone's time and expertise.

The Most Important Role

The **Executive Champion** is by far the most important role on the innovation team. This person is responsible for ensuring that the innovation is aligned with the organization's objectives and strategies. If the innovation is misaligned, then the innovation will be dead on arrival.

More important, the Executive Champion is the person who must inoculate the innovation team against organizational antibodies. The Executive Champion must have a seat at the Management Team table to directly hear and understand the direction that the C-Suite wants to take the organization.

The Executive Champion can leverage this knowledge and insight to anticipate and address the change resistance that's bound to exist. By proactively overcoming objections, the Executive Champion will be able to position your innovation as a vital solution to an important management problem.

No team wins without a strong Executive Champion who stays strong and holds the line against intense opposition.

4. Manage and Eliminate Risk

Ask any venture capitalist or investor about risk and you're bound to hear about three types—concept, product, and execution.

Concept Risk

refers to whether you've got a good idea, i.e., is it desirable?

Product Risk

refers to your ability to build your idea, i.e., is it feasible?

Execution Risk

refers to your organization's ability to deliver your idea, i.e., is it viable?

The IN-90 Framework helps you isolate each type of risk so you can show how you've proactively addressed it. This will increase the confidence of your organization as you reach each milestone on your innovation journey and give executive management the courage to "green light" your innovation.

Tactically, the maps developed during the Desirability stage will validate that you're working on a solution that's causing acute stress with your customers. The MVP prototypes that you create in the Feasibility stage will show the organization what can be built and give you insights on how to minimize product risk. Finally, the cost structure and launch plan maps that you draft during the Viability stage will show what's required to reduce execution risk.

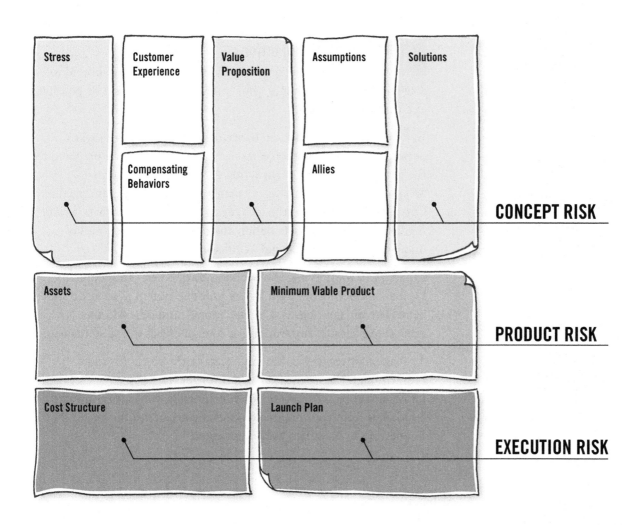

Stress

Customer Experience

Value Proposition

Assumptions

Solutions

Compensating Behaviors

Allies

CONCEPT RISK

Assets

Minimum Viable Product

PRODUCT RISK

Cost Structure

Launch Plan

EXECUTION RISK

Minimizing risk is part of every organization's DNA so recognize it and manage it.

5. Overcome Objections

As long as your organization has people, you're bound to face objections. Any change your innovation creates will be perceived as a threat to someone.

But you have a much better chance of winning the tug of war between innovators and objectors when you are properly prepared for the challenge. David Owens writes in *Creative People Must Be Stopped* that there are six ways organizations try to stop innovation. Organizations object to the idea, design, technology, new sales and marketing demands, distribution and shipping changes, and/or unquantifiable risk (financial, regulatory, legal).

I like to call these types of objections "antibodies." Think about it. Human antibodies are used by the immune system to identify and neutralize foreign objects. Organizational antibodies do the same thing because innovation is a foreign object to the status quo.

To make matters worse, the more foreign the object (or more breakthrough the innovation), the stronger the body (or organization) will respond. Unfortunately, you can't eliminate antibodies from your organization. But you can use the IN-90 Framework to inoculate your innovation.

We live in a culture that makes us do, do, do with an emphasis on moving forward without really considering where we're going.

The Power of Maps

In this book, you will be using maps that will help you find, create, and produce breakthrough innovations. The maps are designed to review what's happening now, help you decide what you'd like to do differently, and instill the energy, drive, and confidence to accelerate from idea to reality.

Maps help you ask and answer tough questions. We live in a culture that makes us do, do, do with an emphasis on moving forward without really considering where we're going. Maps encourage us to stop and ask deep, powerful questions, like:

- What's the real stress?
- What's causing these stresses?
- Is there a much better solution?
- Who can tell us if our solution truly helps?
- Will our solution get people to willingly change?

Maps don't just provide a new view of the landscape. They can also shape your path around, over, or through hazards. For many innovation teams trying to overcome objections, creating a detailed map is the most important thing you can do. Because if you know where the obstacles and hurdles exist within your organization, then you can chart a path that bypasses them.

Maps promote action. If you are paying attention, the visual nature of maps will provoke you to make some fundamental choices that become the basis for action.

- What do we need for our innovation journey?
- What new tools should we try?
- How rapidly can we prototype our ideas?
- How viable is our innovation for our organization?

With the new perspective that maps bring, it's impossible not to make choices and do something—even if you choose to stop working on one innovation and shift resources to another.

MAKE THE MAPS DYNAMIC

Another reason maps are powerful is because they demand interaction from the people using them. The maps in this guide are useless without your input. It is the information you bring to each map that will make it relevant to your innovation effort.

The maps aren't static. You can (and should) revisit each one. You'll likely discover that the maps will have changed. For example, the Desirability maps you create are unlikely to be the same after you build your Feasibility maps and these maps certainly won't be the same after you complete your Viability maps. In fact, revisiting the maps is a useful exercise in itself, since your review can offer new perspectives as well as track the progression of your thinking over time.

USE THE MAPS IN ORDER

There's a method to how the maps are arranged. The maps are designed to build on each other so you can work through them systematically and end up with a specific "Go/No Go" decision on your innovation.

Avoid the temptation to jump to a solution without engaging with the customer first. And use the customer throughout the innovation process as a touch-point to ensure your efforts are staying on track. This will help you overcome senior executives' desire to put their fingerprints on your innovation. You can accept their input, but make it clear you'll need to get feedback to ensure their input is customer-centric.

DON'T WORRY ABOUT BEING PERFECT

You'll never have all the information you need to map out everything fully. And you might find yourself thinking that your map is wrong. Well, of course it is. In fact, there's no such thing as a correct map. Your map is your reality, not someone else's. And your map is only your best guess at describing your reality.

That's okay. One of the reasons why you create a map in the first place is to discover what you don't know, as well as what you do. An incomplete map is useful because often it's the gaps in the map that spark questions and spur you to act.

PREPARATION, I HAVE OFTEN SAID, IS RIGHTLY **TWO THIRDS** OF ANY VENTURE.

— *Amelia Earhart*

BEFORE YOU SET OFF

JOURNEY PREPARATION

PREP MAP 1 — **RISK APPETITE:** Where Are You Today?

PREP MAP 2 — **SET YOUR DIRECTION:** What Don't You Want?

PREP MAP 3 — **INSPIRING PIONEERS:** Who's Great?

PREP MAP 4 — **PASSENGER MANIFEST:** Who's On Your Team?

PREP 1

Where Are You Today?

There's a big idea buried in every assignment.
— George Lois, Original "Mad Man"

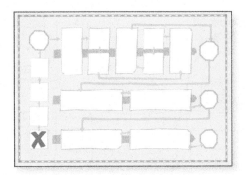

You've seen how powerful the IN-90 Framework can be. You might even imagine how you can use the framework's flexibility to overcome hurdles that tripped you up in the past. And you're eager to get started. But is the IN-90 regimen right for you?

What Works (and What Doesn't)

The IN-90 regimen is an approach to solving problems especially suited to conditions of uncertainty. It is a regimen that manages risk and amplifies rewards through rapid prototyping.

This approach is not suitable for every problem. In many cases, linear methods may work better. For example, if you're facing an operational challenge where the required change is more incremental and where you have good data from the past to predict the future, then you'll be better served with a more traditional analytic method.

The regimen also requires frequent interaction with customers. You must work in an organization that is open-minded to new insights and is willing to challenge industry standard practices. If you find yourself asking what your competitors are doing so you can mimic them, then the regimen is not for you.

Important Definitions

Over the years, I've worked on hundreds of innovation projects and there are three basic types of projects: minor improvements, feature enhancements, and breakthrough innovations.

You probably already know what these terms mean. You live with these types of projects every day. Here are some simple, but important, definitions:

Minor Improvements

Minor improvements are the things you do to increase efficiency or streamline processes. You probably spend most of your time on minor improvements because they are safe, risk-averse adjustments to an existing operation.

Minor improvements come from your education, your training, and the culture of your organization, particularly if you work for a manufacturing, distribution, or retailing organization. These improvements are usually considered successful if they reduce cost, improve margins, or enhance compliance.

Feature Enhancements

Feature enhancements provide new functionality or capability to existing processes. There's a range of feature enhancements: at one end, it's interesting work, and you can quantify the improvements you've made; at the other, it is more mundane, but you recognize its necessity.

For example, when Amazon.com offered One-Click shopping and Prime shipping, the company could quantify the improvements made. When Amazon.com offered the features of Your Recommendations and Your Wish List, these enhancements were necessary to improve the shopping experience, but didn't produce measurable change.

Breakthrough Innovations

Breakthrough innovations are the lifeblood of all organizations. They inspire, stretch, and provoke. Breakthroughs are the innovations that matter—to your organization and to you.

For organizations, breakthrough innovations drive strategic difference, profit, and market share. It is the kind of work that pushes businesses forward, engages people with a newfound spirit of optimism, and makes a meaningful difference to your customers.

For you, breakthrough innovations represent a source of deep comfort and engagement—often you feel as though you're in the "zone" where you're working at your best, effortlessly. You're in alignment with your aspirations for the impact you want to have on the world—and what you're doing may actually be FUN!

Many organizations claim that they want to be as innovative as Apple or Google. But do they really?

Apple and Google have HUGE appetites for risk and change. For example, when they release a new Operating System, it impacts every new and existing device, every internal and third party software application, and every country in the world!

Remember that this map is meant for you. So don't worry if your innovation initiatives don't match up to others. Think about what represents a breakthrough innovation for your organization, industry, or market. That's all that really matters.

Completing Prep Map 1

1. Divide the circle into three pie slices representing how many minor improvements, feature enhancements, and breakthrough innovations you are considering.
    Trust your intuition on this—you don't have to be overly precise. And, by the way, the proportions are almost certainly not one third each.

2. Write down two or three examples of each type of innovation in each segment.
    This will help you substantiate the size of each slice of pie.

3. Circle the one breakthrough innovation you want to pursue.
    This will be the initiative you'll map out through the remainder of this guide.

Prep Map 1: Risk Appetite

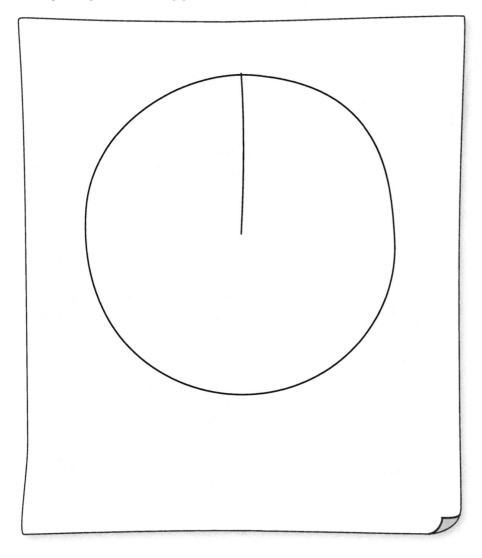

Getting Insights from Prep Map 1

1. **Write down how your current mix makes you feel.**
    What are you happy about? What are you disappointed about?

2. **Why do you think your current mix looks like this?**
    Do you need new capabilities? Do you need a better link to your organization's objectives and strategies? Do you need greater executive involvement?

3. **What would your ideal mix be?** How would you like the map to look? This "gap analysis"—where you are now and where you want to go—will help you understand what you need to change on your map.

Debriefing Prep Map 1

Creating the map is a good thing, but the real learning comes when you take a minute or two to debrief. To help you recognize and remember your insights, answer these questions:

- What's the main thing you noticed from this map?

- What, if anything, surprised you? Was it the amount of incremental improvements? Was it the number of breakthrough innovations?

- What are the characteristics of each type of innovation? How are they alike? How are they different?

- What do you know now that you didn't know before?

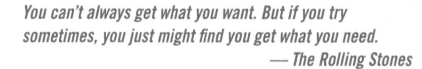

PREP 2

SET YOUR DIRECTION
What Don't You Want?

You can't always get what you want. But if you try sometimes, you just might find you get what you need.
— *The Rolling Stones*

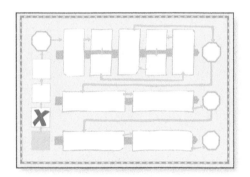

Now that you've looked at all the projects you are considering, it's time to focus on the single breakthrough innovation journey you want to take.

Framing and scoping an innovation is critical for effectively pursuing breakthrough innovations. And when you don't have a handle on the customer dynamics (and you won't at this point), this can be a real challenge. But knowing what you don't want can unleash what you need.

When you take this approach, you're able to put a stake in the ground and say, "This is where we're starting from. We know we'll change direction as we learn more, but this is what we know today."

Inspiration From Fear

It's often hard to know what you want. So don't spend a lot of time trying to envision a future that is yet to be imagined. Instead, focus your efforts on describing what you don't want. Your fears are often close to the surface, while your desires are often buried deep.

For example, most people struggle to find a new job because they don't know what they want. But if you ask them what they don't want in a new job, the words flow effortlessly. If you don't want to be tied down in an office, don't like routine, don't want to be paid the same as someone who doesn't work as hard as you, but don't want to build a business infrastructure from scratch, then you might want to be an insurance agent, real estate agent, or business broker.

By defining what you don't want, you've uncovered what you might want. In all likelihood, you probably never considered being something like an insurance agent because you hadn't uncovered the insight that really drives you. The same dynamic is true when you're thinking about your innovation.

Completing Prep Map 2

1. **Write down twenty things you don't want to happen when you launch your innovation.** These things can describe how customers feel or think about your product or service. They can also describe the marketing, sales, distribution, delivery or post-sale process. Don't censor yourself—just jot down the things that come to mind. You'll have a chance to edit later.

2. **Think of a worst-case scenario.** Add another ten things to your list. Some will be a variation on the twenty you already have and that's fine, but also try to find some new words.

3. **Now narrow your list down to the ten words that are the biggest disasters you can imagine.** They should be the ten that seem to best sum up when things are really breaking down, when you're having the least impact, when things are really screwing up.

4. **Now it's time for the second part of the map.** We're going to complete the other column. You're looking for words or metaphors that capture a new way of executing the customer experience.

5. **Pick one word in the left-hand column you've already completed.** Now find a word, metaphor, or real-world example that describes what you'd like your customer to experience. The word won't necessarily be the literal or extreme opposite of the partner word in the left-hand column. So the partner to "complex process" might not be "eliminate process" but "two-step process." The secret to making this column work is to have words that recognize that not all constraints can be completely erased. For example, auto manufacturers might have big problems with their dealerships, but it's unrealistic to operate without them.

6. **Just as you did with the words in the first column, play around and tweak these words.** The goal is to find the most powerful, most accurate way to describe the ideal customer experience.

Prep Map 2: Set Your Course

I DON'T want this:	But I DO want this:

Getting Insights from Prep Map 2

1. **Once you have a set of words that works for you, create two sets of copies.** Make one copy large enough for a conference room to use when the entire innovation team meets. Make a second notebook-sized, laminated copy for individual innovation team members to carry from meeting to meeting.

2. **Keep working with your list.** I've found you can quickly get it to 80 percent right—pairs of words that do a pretty good job of capturing the not this/this dichotomy—but sometimes revisiting and tweaking the words can help bring other people on board and make this list even more focused and relevant.

Debriefing Prep Map 2

Capture what you've learned from this map by answering the following questions:

▸ What's the main thing you noticed from this map?

▸ When you scan the words in the left-hand column, what do you feel? What do you think? What does that tell you?

▸ When you scan the words in the right-hand column, what do you feel? What do you think? What does that tell you?

▸ What do you know now that you hadn't fully realized before?

It's a rough road that leads to the heights of greatness.
— Lucius Annaeus Seneca, Roman Philosopher

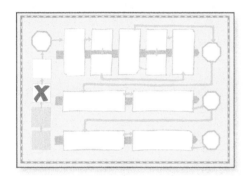

We've all revered some product, service, or solution at some time or another. You stop and wonder, "How'd they do that?" or "That's really clever" or maybe just "I REALLY like that!"

These days we aren't fooled by what's said, and we look for actions. If you tap into the behaviors of your heroes, then you'll understand what inspires you. You can then take these guiding principles to your innovation team.

Why Do You Feel Good?

This map will focus on asking, "What is it about this company that I most admire? What's best about what they do? What really makes them great?"

Your sources of inspiration can be famous or not, for profit or not, public or not. Scan your experiences, and think about what captured your imagination (for example, Tesla's 100% electric cars), events you've always held in high esteem (for example, TED Talks), or a company or organization you think does great work (for example, Habitat For Humanity). Understanding what or who inspires you will lead to a fountain of energy that can refresh and renew your spirit.

Completing Prep Map 3

1. **Think of products, services or companies you think are inspiring for one reason or another.** They should be things you'd like to own, experiences you'd like to have, services you'd like to enjoy, or organizations with whom you'd like to be affiliated.

2. **Create a list of five products or services or companies that you think are great.** Choose the five you feel are the most compelling, about whom you'd be most likely to say, "Yes, I'd like us to embody what they've got," and write one name per box in the left-hand column of the map.

3. **For each product, service, or company, list four things they do that inspired you.** These should be behaviors exhibited, qualities you sense, or situations they have created. Dig deep. If you like Apple technology, ask, "Why is that important to you?" Write down your answer and ask, "And why is that important to you?" Continue the process until you capture the essence of what it is that makes you feel good about the product, service or solution.

Prep Map 3: Inspiring Pioneers

Who's Great?	What do they do?
	1. 2. 3. 4.
	1. 2. 3. 4.
	1. 2. 3. 4.
	1. 2. 3. 4.
	1. 2. 3. 4.

Getting Insights from Prep Map 3

1. **Look for patterns in your map.** Recurring themes or words can give you a clue about what you believe is important, how you'd like to shape your innovation, and where you can find analogous examples to explain your vision to others.

2. **If you feel uncertain about your next move or get stuck in the bureaucracy of your own organization, ask yourself:**

   ► What would (insert great organization) do?

   ► How would (insert great organization) overcome this hurdle?

   Doing this might help you get out of your current mindset and reveal alternative ways to approach the situation.

Debriefing Prep Map 3

Capture what you've learned from this map by answering the following questions:

- What was most powerful about listing who's great?

- Who surprised you by showing up on your list? What surprised you?

- What characteristic showed up that your organization already has and you take for granted?

- What's become clearer about where you are and where you want to go?

PREP 4

PASSENGER MANIFEST
Who's On Your Team?

Where we all think alike, no one thinks very much.
— *Walter Lippmann, Author*

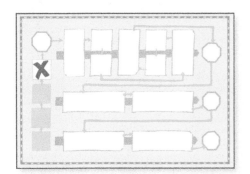

People usually like to surround themselves with similar people. Your friends often share similar interests. Your work colleagues frequently share similar viewpoints. Even your neighbors share similar concerns.

But this is one of the paradoxes of innovation. Breakthrough innovations inspire you, enthrall you, and engage you—it's deeply personal. And yet, you can't innovate by yourself. You need a diverse set of people with unique skills to turn your idea into reality. After all, a team without diversity is just a peer group.

The good news is that with some searching, you'll find all the help you need. More important, you'll be able to figure out who can provide the creative skills, political support, and even opposing points of view that you need to consider. And you'll know exactly what you need everybody to do, so it'll be easy to ask people to join your innovation team.

Outside In

Many organizations seek to align themselves with people who "know the industry." And there's some value to that knowledge because you need to work with people who understand the operating levers of a business, i.e., who does what in your value chain, how you go to market, and how you get paid.

But you have to be careful not to be too insular. Look for people outside your organization that have experience launching new

products and services. Seek outside people who know how to overcome internal obstacles. Include outside people that have faced the tough questions asked by senior executives and customers alike.

Adopting this "Outside In" approach will help you get objective counsel and advice. It also allows you the freedom to be more innovative because you're leveraging business models, innovation techniques, and marketing strategies from other industries.

Completing Prep Map 4

1. **People with influence.** They can give you resources, provide political cover, and connect you with people whose help you need.

2. **People with "T-shaped" (deep and wide) skills.** These are people who have deep technical, systemic expertise as well as wide cross-industry expertise. They are equally right-brained and left-brained. They are the rare combination of out-of-the-box thinkers who know how to produce scalable results.

3. **People who might oppose you.** Don't underestimate how important these people can be to you. They are likely to block your innovation down the road so you should make them part of the solution today.

4. **People who will fight for you.** There has never been a breakthrough innovation that did not have an Executive Champion fighting and defeating the organizational antibodies. You need one person that passionately believes in your innovation and will tie their success to yours.

Prep Map 4: Passenger Manifest

People With Influence	WHO?	How can they help?	How will you ask?
Product Owner		Complete Map 1: Stress	
Customer Service Representative		Complete Map 2: Customer Experience	
Storyteller		Complete Map 7: Value Proposition	

People With Skills	WHO?	How can they help?	How will you ask?
Business Solutions Architect		Complete Map 4: Solutions	
Project Manager		Complete Map 5: Assumptions	
Innovation Team Leader		Complete Map 8: Assets	
Prototype Experimenter		Complete Map 9: Minimum Viable Product	
User Experience Architect		Complete Map 6: Allies	
Marketing Manager		Complete Map 11: Launch Plan	

People Who Might Oppose You	WHO?	How can they help?	How will you ask?
Sales Manager or Operations Manager		Complete Map 3: Compensating Behaviors	
Finance Manager		Complete Map 10: Cost Structure	

People Who Will Fight For You	WHO?	How can they help?	How will you ask?
Executive Champion		Serve & protect you in Senior Executive Meetings	

Getting Insights from Prep Map 4

1. **Look for themes in your map.** Are there certain internal or external people you absolutely need to get onboard? Why are they so critical? Are there any substitutes?

2. **Where are you vulnerable?** Do you lack influence, skills, or opposition people? What can you do about these gaps?

Debriefing Prep Map 4

Capture what you've learned from this map by answering the following questions:

- How diverse is your innovation team? Do you feel it is diverse enough? Why or why not?

- How do you feel about working with such a diverse team? What excites you about the team? What worries you?

- Do you feel you have the right skilled people? Do these skilled people have enough time to dedicate to your innovation?

- When senior executives ask about the composition of your team, how well do you feel you have your bases covered?

YOUR PROJECT CHARTER

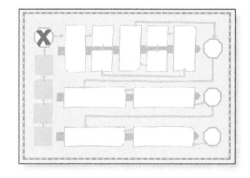

You can't wait for inspiration. You have to go after it with a club. — Jack London, Author

A typical Project Charter is a statement of the scope, objectives, and participants in a project. If your Project Charter is well written, it will tell you two things — what you know and what you don't know. It is between the space of the known and unknown that you'll find inspiration.

Spend time carefully thinking through your Project Charter because even though your project is likely to be full of uncertainty, your Project Charter doesn't need to be. It should be concise and simple so any one who reads it will understand the questions you're asking and why they're important.

You can't eliminate uncertainty because some key elements regarding your innovation won't be known upfront. That's why it's even more important to drive ambiguity out of the Project Charter. You want to provide as much clarity, control, and transparency as possible to build the confidence of your decision makers.

LESS IS MORE

You should limit the Project Charter to one page so it's easy to understand and can be updated as you learn more. This document will be useful for keeping important stakeholders (your boss, cross-functional leaders, partners) informed about your innovation project as it progresses.

Completing Your Project Charter

1. **Take out your Prep Maps 1–4.** Review all of the maps to make sure they are updated with the most current information.

2. **Look for consistency across the maps.** What themes or trends or dynamics do you see in your maps? Do you have language that reflects the insights you've discovered? Is that language on your maps?

3. **Create a name for your project.** This should be a description that is easy to understand, and memorable. Be careful not to describe what you think the final innovation might be. If you're wrong (and you probably will be), then you'll have to explain the difference between your project charter and your final innovation.

4. **Cut and paste sections from your Prep Maps.**
   Prep Map 2: I Don't Want This
   Establish the guardrails for your innovation by listing what you don't want.
   Prep Map 2: I Do Want This
   Determine the direction for your innovation by referring to what you do want.
   Prep Map 3: Who's Great
   Select the evaluation criteria you admire and want to use for your innovation.
   Prep Map 4: Who's On Your Team
   List your innovation team members according to the role they will play.

Milestone 1: Project Charter

Project Name:	*Date:*
Executive Champion: (Insert Prep Map 4 Executive Champion here)	*Innovation Team Leader:* (Insert Prep Map 4 Innovation Team Leader here)

Guardrails: What do you want to avoid?
(Insert left-hand column of Prep Map 2: "I DON'T Want This" here)

Direction: What do you want to happen?
(Insert right hand column of Prep Map 2: "But I DO Want This" here)

Innovation Evaluation Criteria: How will you measure success?
(Insert items from Prep Map 3: Who's Great? What do they do? here)

Team Members:	List Team Members (Insert Prep Map 4: Who's On Your Team here)
Product Owner	
Customer Service Representative	
Sales Manager or Operations Manager	
Business Solutions Architect	
User Experience Architect	
Project Manager	
Storyteller	
Prototype Experimenter	
Finance Manager	
Marketing Manager	

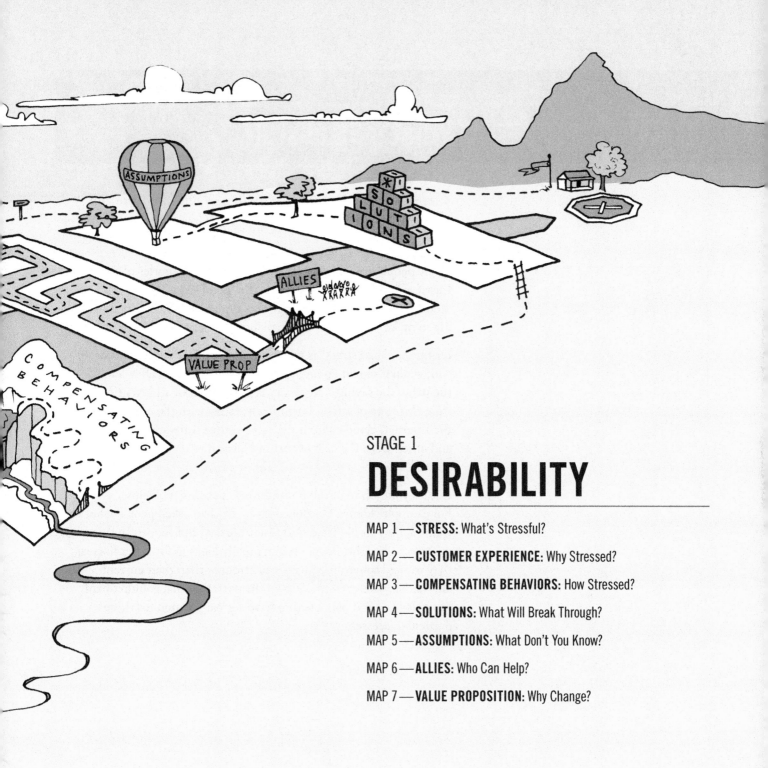

STAGE 1

DESIRABILITY

MAP 1 — **STRESS:** What's Stressful?

MAP 2 — **CUSTOMER EXPERIENCE:** Why Stressed?

MAP 3 — **COMPENSATING BEHAVIORS:** How Stressed?

MAP 4 — **SOLUTIONS:** What Will Break Through?

MAP 5 — **ASSUMPTIONS:** What Don't You Know?

MAP 6 — **ALLIES:** Who Can Help?

MAP 7 — **VALUE PROPOSITION:** Why Change?

MAP 1

STRESS
What's Stressful?

Chains of habit are too light to be felt until they are too heavy to be broken. — *Warren Buffet, Investor*

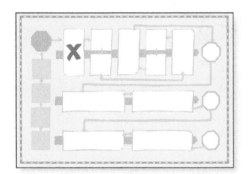

Many people are unaware that there are two categories of stress: Eustress and Distress. Eustress is the "good stress" that motivates you to keep working. This type of stress is needed in your life to make you feel happy, challenged, and productive.

Distress or "bad stress" is when tension builds, there's frustration, and, when it's great enough, you'll do something to alleviate the pain. The saying, "Necessity is the mother of all invention" comes from this type of stress. Fortunately, today with the advent of the Internet, cloud computing, open source software, 3-D printing and other tools, the cost of turning ideas into reality is at an all-time low.

But it's your job to develop insight into people's problems. For example, Henry Ford once said, "If I had asked people what they wanted, they would have said faster horses." But hidden in this quote is an insight: People weren't really looking for faster horses; they wanted something faster and stronger than their current alternative. The stress was slow transportation that couldn't haul heavy loads. Ford happened to have a great solution for these particular stresses.

Beware Indifference

So what's stressing your prospective customers? What's making them really angry? More important, what's making them indifferent to your organization? And why? After all, you don't want them to merely "accept" your product or service; you want them to "prefer" your product or service.

Many organizations can usually find out what's stressing their existing customers by looking at their internal customer satisfaction metrics. But these numbers only scratch the surface. You need to observe people in their "natural habitat" to understand what job they are trying to do. Only then can you deeply emphasize and understand how to help. There's no other substitute.

Completing Map 1

1. **Name ten stresses your prospective customers (either internal or external) experience.** Be as specific as you can. The more clearly you can articulate these stresses, the more clearly opportunities for innovation will become apparent.

2. **Name ten more stresses.** The first list you created will often trigger deeper more painful issues. Think of the first list as the symptoms and the second list as the root cause(s) of the symptoms.

3. **Now explore the impact of these stresses.** When these stresses occur, what happens behaviorally? Emotionally?

4. **Finally, what do these behaviors and emotions tell you?** What key insight have you discovered?

Map 1: Stress

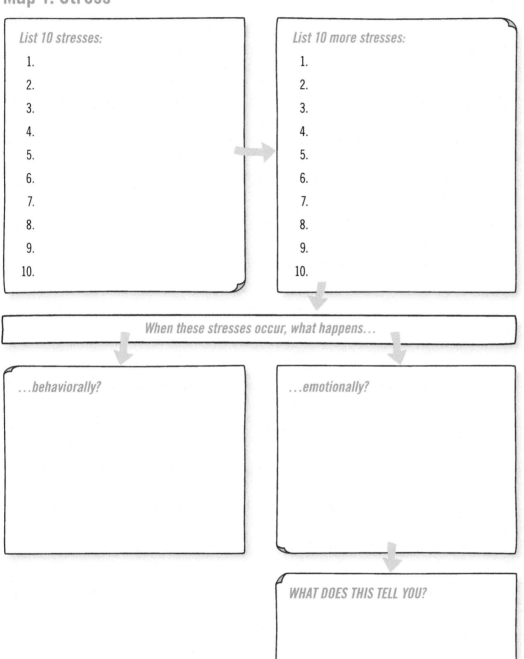

List 10 stresses:

1.
2.
3.
4.
5.
6.
7.
8.
9.
10.

List 10 more stresses:

1.
2.
3.
4.
5.
6.
7.
8.
9.
10.

When these stresses occur, what happens…

…behaviorally?

…emotionally?

WHAT DOES THIS TELL YOU?

Getting Insights from Map 1

1. **Look for themes in your map.** Are there certain patterns you notice? What's the root cause of these stresses? Why do they occur?

2. **Look for major stress points.** Are there certain stresses you absolutely need to take care of? Why are they so critical?

3. **How do these stresses affect your prospective customers?** What is the cost of these stresses? Who has to pay for them? How can you measure the cost?

4. **How do competitors handle these stresses?** Is there an opportunity to create a competitive advantage for your organization by addressing critical stress points?

Debriefing Map 1

Capture what you've learned from this map by answering the following questions:

▸ What's the most interesting thing you noticed from this map?

▸ As you moved through the stresses, where did your energy or excitement or interest increase? Where did it drop?

▸ What is the cost if nothing changes? How can you quantitatively measure this cost?

▸ Is there any connection between the various things that need to change? Is there an overall pattern?

▸ What do you know about your prospective customers that you hadn't fully realized before?

How do we even know these are customer stresses?

Like anthropologists, we observed customers in their native environment.

MAP 2

CUSTOMER EXPERIENCE
Why Stressed?

They may call you doctor or they may call you chief, but you're gonna have to serve somebody.
— Bob Dylan, Music Mystic

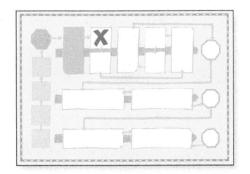

Now that you know *what* is stressful, it's time to understand more about *why* these stresses are occurring. Is it because of how people or things are (or are not) happening directly "On Stage?" Or is it because people or things are (or are not) working "Back Stage?"

For example, if your airline flight is delayed, is the gate agent keeping you informed? Is he sympathetic? Helpful? Or is the gate agent, despite being helpful and sympathetic, lacking critical information about the status of your flight? In other words, are the "Back Stage" systems failing to serve the gate agent who is "On Stage" so he, in turn, is failing to serve you?

Journey Mapping

Journey mapping is the diagnostic tool we'll use to dig deeper into prospective customer stresses. Journey mapping allows us to represent, in flowchart format, the actual experience of receiving a product or service.

When you use journey mapping, it's important to map the actual experience—not what you want it to be or what you think it should be. If you use journey mapping correctly, it will remove more risk from your innovation than any other activity.

That's because organizations often misjudge or misunderstand what customers want. But mapping forces you to shift your focus from "what does my organization want?" to "what job is my prospective customer trying to do?"

Completing Map 2

1. **Lay out your understanding of what a customer's journey looks like from beginning to end.** Be sure to include all the steps in the journey, not just the ones in which your organization participates.

2. **List the people and things your customer interacts with directly.** This will help you understand the work that is being done and how value is either being enhanced or diminished in the customer experience.

3. **Now list the people and things that are working behind the scenes.** This will help you understand the work that is being done (usually by technology) to support the people and things directly interacting with your customer.

4. **Go through each step of the customer journey and circle the steps that a third-party (e.g., distributor, retailer, call center) controls.** This will help you outline where your sphere of influence on the journey begins and ends. Perhaps you'll want to change substantial steps in the journey if your organization or a third-party is better suited to enhance the customer experience.

Map 2: Customer Experience

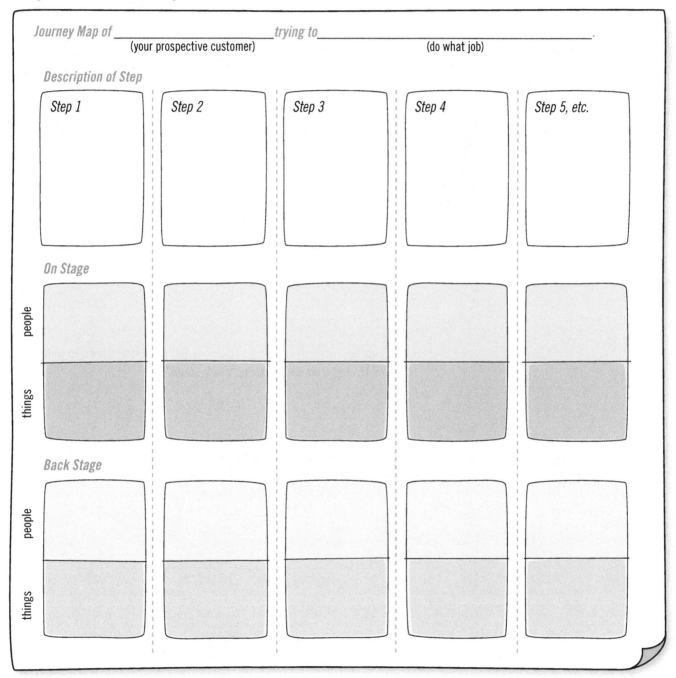

Journey Map of _____ trying to_____ .
(your prospective customer)   (do what job)

Description of Step

| Step 1 | Step 2 | Step 3 | Step 4 | Step 5, etc. |

On Stage

people

things

Back Stage

people

things

Getting Insights from Map 2

1. **Look at each step in the journey.** How many steps create a positive experience? How many steps result in a negative experience?

2. **Look for stress triggers "on stage."** Are there certain people or things that cause stress "on stage"?

3. **Look for stress triggers "back stage."** Are there certain people or things that cause stress "back stage"?

Debriefing Map 2

Recognize and remember your insights by answering the following questions:

▸ What did you learn by focusing on the big picture? What surprised you?

▸ What were the obvious opportunities for innovation?

▸ What were less obvious opportunities for innovation?

▸ What do you know now about your customer's journey that you hadn't fully realized before?

How do we know what's causing the stress?

We mapped the customer experience to identify the root causes of stress.

MAP 3

COMPENSATING BEHAVIORS
How Stressed?

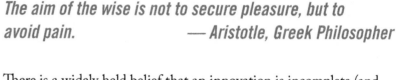

The aim of the wise is not to secure pleasure, but to avoid pain. — *Aristotle, Greek Philosopher*

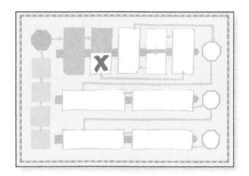

There is a widely held belief that an innovation is incomplete (and, therefore, flawed) unless it alleviates every stress. The problem with this belief is that it leads to two things that stop innovation in its tracks — management indecision and scope creep.

You can easily see how this happens. You've probably been in meetings where a new idea or innovation is being presented and unless it solves the problems and pains of everyone in the room, it's going nowhere. So, in an act of desperation, the innovation team offers to add features and functionality to address everyone's issues.

The result is a bloated, complex innovation that is difficult to sell, support, and maintain. And this assumes the innovation team is able to keep the project alive even though the project will be over budget and miss key milestones.

What's important is to fix the big things that are broken or causing acute pain. A brilliant creative director on Madison Avenue once told me, "You never get credit for doing more than three things. So pick the three things that matter most and do them well. Exceptionally well."

Normalizing Emotion

Until recently, there weren't adequate tools to communicate about emotion. But two things were known about emotion—it vacillates and it's difficult to describe.

The next map will help you map how emotion vacillates from high to neutral to low. At each point of vacillation, you'll be asked to describe each emotional state. If people are in real pain, they are likely to exhibit compensating behaviors. These compensating behaviors are sometimes described as "work arounds" or "temporary fixes" or "patches."

But in some cases, there may not be many practical ways to avoid pain. (Think about filing your taxes or buying a car.) Here's where getting out and talking to people helps most.

Perhaps stresses are alleviated by procrastinating, or asking others for advice, or trying to delegate, or by doing nothing—the ultimate pain avoidance strategy.

Completing Map 3

1. **Look at the Customer Journey you created in Map 2.**
   For each step in the journey, assess the emotional state of your prospective customer. For example, if someone is shopping online, they might experience an emotional high when they find what they're looking for, but might experience an emotional low when it comes time to check out.

2. **Pick a point on the emotion scale for each step in the journey.**
   Then spend some time thinking about what specifically is the source of this emotion.

3. **Next, use an adjective to describe each emotional state.**
   The points on the emotion scale and the adjectives you select should be consistent.

4. **Finally, select the three most negative emotional steps in the journey.** Identify what compensating behaviors are exhibited (if any) to alleviate these negative experiences.

Map 3: Compensating Behaviors

Journey Map of _____ trying to _____.
(your prospective customer)   (complete what job)

Description of Step

| Step 1 | Step 2 | Step 3 | Step 4 | Step 5 |

Emotional State

	Step 1	Step 2	Step 3	Step 4	Step 5
EUPHORIC +10					
HAPPY +8					
PLEASED +6					
CONTENT +4					
SATISFIED +2					
INDIFFERENT 0					
DISSATISFIED -2					
DISCONTENT -4					
DISPLEASED -6					
UNHAPPY -8					
ANGRY -10					

Adjective: _____

Emotional Level:

Compensating Behaviors

Who:

Compensates by:

Getting Insights from Map 3

1. **Look at the emotional dynamics of the customer journey.** How much does the emotional experience vacillate?

2. **Look at the emotional high.** What people or things are causing the emotional highs?

3. **Look at the emotional lows.** What people or things are causing the emotional lows?

4. **Look at the compensating behaviors.** How likely is it that these behaviors make your customer indifferent, or even hostile?

Debriefing Map 3

Reflect on what you've discovered by answering the following questions:

▸ What did you learn from the pattern of emotional highs and lows?

▸ What emotional highs can you leverage as competitive points of differentiation?

▸ What emotional lows must be addressed immediately?

▸ How do you feel about the emotional dynamics of your customer?

What makes you think these stresses are bothering customers?

We learned how our customers must compensate for our shortcomings.

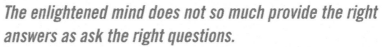

MAP 4

SOLUTIONS
What Will Break Through?

The enlightened mind does not so much provide the right answers as ask the right questions.
—Claude Levi-Strauss, Anthropologist

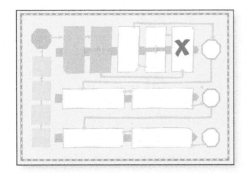

Brainstorming sessions can be either powerful, insightful experiences or dispiriting, soul-draining time wasters. When the call goes out, "Let's brainstorm this," some hearts rise and others sink. People walk into the meeting room, and walk out a couple of hours later with a few new ideas, but rarely is the entire group inspired to move ahead enthusiastically.

Why does this happen? It's usually a combination of three things. You've got the wrong people, the wrong process, and the wrong questions.

Let's start with the people. Often the people in the room are being asked to do something they're not comfortable doing. For example, if you work for a large organization, you've probably got a lot of excellent operators in the room. These people know if things are running as expected and can handle the unexpected with existing processes and procedures, but they're usually not "out of the box" thinkers.

Even if you have people that are comfortable thinking outside the box, they usually can't afford to give enough time and space to have new ideas. They're busy keeping up with the tasks at hand, and it's hard to stop, focus, and create the relaxed free time the process of breakthrough innovations require.

But most important, the right questions are rarely asked. Without the right questions, you can generate "blue sky" ideas that can't be executed. Or you can generate a series of incremental improvements, bundle them together, and call it "innovation." Either way, you're off track.

Mental Preparation

This map is designed to ask some powerful and provocative questions. The first thing to do is shift gears mentally. Generating ideas in a focused way is not something you probably do regularly, so you might find it frustrating. Think of creativity as a muscle and recognize that it might not be as strong as you'd like it to be.

Remember, you don't need to edit or sensor your ideas. In fact, I encourage you to have ideas that are improbable, impossible, illegal, or irresponsible. This isn't about deciding what you're going to be doing; it's just about stretching your mind. And often the slightly insane ideas open the door for some more interesting (and sane) ones.

Bear in mind that you don't actually have to do any of these ideas. Having the idea isn't a commitment to action. This gives you the freedom to let your mind wander, knowing it's okay to generate ideas that are difficult or even impossible to implement.

Completing Map 4

1. **Review your list of stresses to focus your efforts.**
   Give yourself a time limit to have ideas and set a goal for that time limit. Try for 15 ideas in 5 minutes. This prohibits criticism of your ideas and focuses your brain on production, not evaluation.

2. **Start at the top of the map with, "What ideas do you already have?"** This allows you to capture the current thoughts you have for alleviating stresses. These ideas might be big and bold or small and tactical. They might be very specific or fairly abstract. You may also find that listing the ideas you already have leads to new ones. Write them all down. Keep going until you run out of ideas.

3. **Now you're ready for some *new* ideas.** Scan the remaining questions and pick one that strikes your fancy. Use it to generate another 15 ideas in 5 minutes.

4. **Pick a second question and do the same thing.**
   Generate another 15 ideas in 5 minutes.

5. **Continue the process until you've answered all the questions.**
   Be sure to generate 15 ideas in 5 minutes for each question.

6. **Pick your favorite three or four ideas and then generate additional questions for each idea you select.** This will help you tap into the rhythm of creativity—focusing on what's best and then expanding on what's possible. One way to do this is to speak out loud the idea you've already had and add, "This makes me think of…"

Map 4: Solutions

What ideas do you have already?

What's the most efficient thing to do?

What's the easiest thing to do?

What's the fastest thing to do?

What's the industry-leading thing to do?

What's the provocative thing to do?

Getting Insights from Map 4

1. **Review all of the ideas you've written down.**
   Don't worry if you don't think you've found an idea that
   will break through. You've expanded what's possible,
   and you've created a backlog of ideas to take to people
   for validation. That's a great result.

2. **Look closely at the ideas that are most interesting to you.**
   For each idea ask, "What would we need to make this idea
   a reality?" Pay attention to the ones that look most interesting to
   you, but don't rush into choosing the ones that you'll pursue.
   At this point, you have enough to mold into simple statements
   of "What if?"

Debriefing Map 4

Let the lessons of the map sink in by answering these questions:

- What was it like to review the ideas you already had?
  Did you have more or fewer ideas than you thought?

- Which were your favorite new questions? What does that
  say to you?

- Was this process difficult or easy for you? Why do you think you
  felt this way?

- Did you notice a tendency to evaluate the ideas as they were
  created? What is that saying about your ability to generate ideas?
  What does it say about how you react to other people's ideas?

How do you know THIS is the best solution?

We used "T-shaped" thinking to look across industries and deep into operational details.

MAP 5

If we all worked on the assumption that what is accepted as true is really true, there would be little hope of advancement. — *Orville Wright, Aviation Innovator*

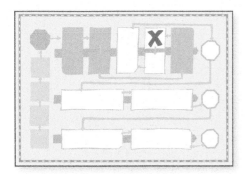

Every innovation begins as a guess about what people desire and what they will *value*. By completing the maps you've tackled so far, you've changed a guessing game into a well-informed, structured experiment.

Like any experiment, your innovation is built on some underlying assumptions about what will make your innovation compelling enough to change behavior. Now is the time to articulate these assumptions so when you test them you'll gain confidence in your innovation's likelihood of success.

Pass/Fail

Well-constructed assumptions identify the 'pass/fail' elements of your innovation. Creating your Assumptions Map involves taking a hard look at the maps you've already completed and honestly assessing whether your proposed solution will sufficiently alleviate the stresses you've identified.

You must drill down to the core assumptions upon which your innovation depends. When you lay out these core assumptions, you'll be specifying the tests your innovation must "pass" in order to be successful.

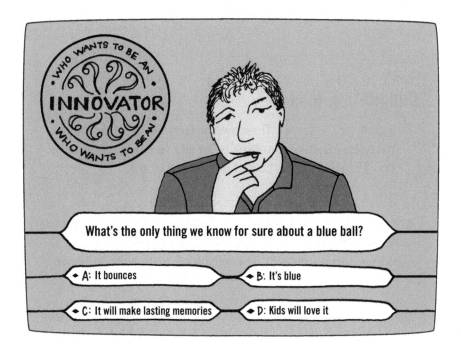

For example, let's say you're considering an application that creates a checklist of daily reminders for the elderly (e.g., take prescription medicines, do physical therapy, get a car oil change, send a birthday card). You know from well-documented clinical research that the elderly often struggle to be compliant with medical protocol, need to stay active physically, and need to interact with other people.

What you don't know, but could know is how many people over 65 use smartphones, tablets, computers, email, and even Facebook. These are facts that you can find out. But what you don't know and can't know is whether the elderly will continue to use the service over time. This is something you'll have to learn by tracking behaviors and making adjustments, e.g., creating reports for caregivers to monitor usage, after your innovation gets into the marketplace.

Completing Map 5

1. **List what you know.** These are the facts, as you know them today. Be careful not to list a belief as a fact; don't confuse the two. When in doubt, keep it out of the fact list.

2. **List what you don't know and can't know.** This is what you can't know without a crystal ball. No amount of testing can resolve this uncertainty. The only thing to do here is predict.

3. **List what you don't know but could.** In any innovation, there is a lot that you could know, but you haven't had the time to go get the data.

4. **Figure out how you could quickly get the data for what you don't know but could.** Sometimes this will involve trade data, sometimes it will require internal data, and other times you'll need competitive data. Remember, managers love data because it gives them confidence, so find it if you can.

Map 5: Assumptions

Facts We Know	Facts We Don't Know but COULD know	Facts We Don't Know and CAN'T Know
	We could quickly gather data by:	

Getting Insights from Map 5

1. **What percentage of things do you know compared to what you don't know?** The percentage of what you don't know should be much higher than what you know. Otherwise, you're probably working on an incremental improvement rather than an innovation.

2. **What are the characteristics of the things you don't know and can't know?** These assumptions should be macro issues like adoption rates or sales velocity. You can make some estimates, but you need to recognize that you won't really know the answer until you get your innovation launched.

3. **How quickly can you realistically get data for what you don't know but could?** Between the Internet, social media, and a well-placed phone call, you'll be surprised about how much you can uncover. Most people want to help, but you have to ask.

Debriefing Map 5

Review what you've learned from this map by answering the
following questions:

▸ What surprised you the most about your list of assumptions?

▸ What do you think you know now about your key factors
of success that you didn't realize before?

▸ What critically important assumptions must you test to build
the confidence of your organization?

▸ How do you think your confidence will be affected after you
test your assumptions?

MAP 6

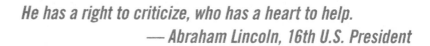

Who Can Help?

He has a right to criticize, who has a heart to help.
— Abraham Lincoln, 16th U.S. President

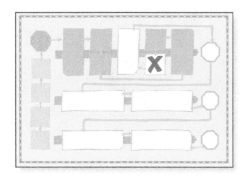

At a minimum, great customers or power users will validate or refute your assumptions. But you'll know the real value of a great customer or power user when, in a moment of insight, you say to yourself, "Yes, this is something to remember. This is a key insight that's essential for our innovation to succeed."

The fundamental flaw of most innovation efforts is that they fail to collaborate with customers or prospects. Too often innovations are conceived and developed inside the four walls of a building. These efforts are usually shrouded in secrecy until the "grand reveal" at an executive meeting or even a sales conference.

Here's the problem with this approach. These types of innovation efforts frequently focus on features, technological wizardry, or (even worse) claims that can be easily dismissed like, "this will make things easier for you" or "we're here to help" or "risk-free, worry-free." None of these statements will engage a person's heart and encourage them to adopt your innovation.

So how can you enlist help early in the innovation process? What will compel people to come to your aid? What will motivate them to work side-by-side with you? What will make them your innovation's advocates?

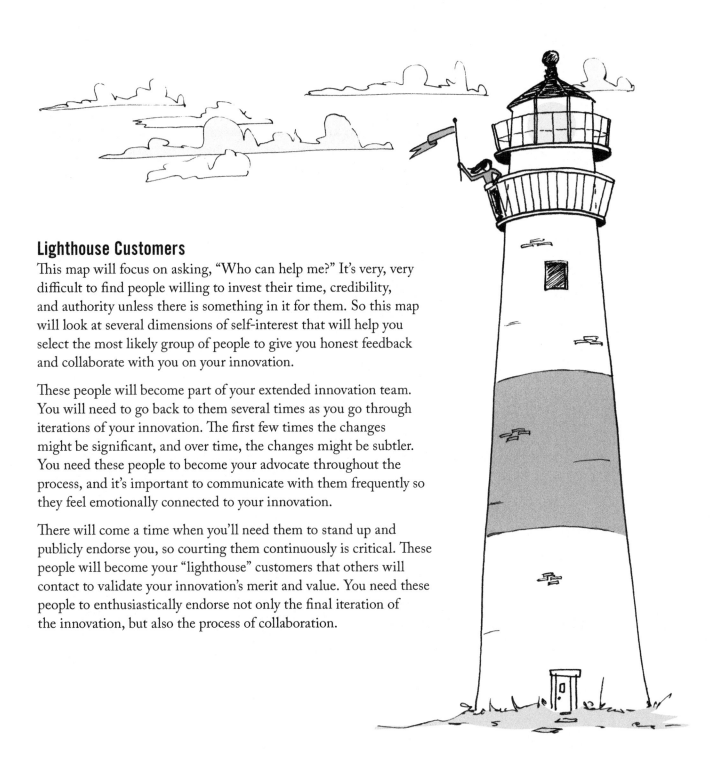

Lighthouse Customers

This map will focus on asking, "Who can help me?" It's very, very difficult to find people willing to invest their time, credibility, and authority unless there is something in it for them. So this map will look at several dimensions of self-interest that will help you select the most likely group of people to give you honest feedback and collaborate with you on your innovation.

These people will become part of your extended innovation team. You will need to go back to them several times as you go through iterations of your innovation. The first few times the changes might be significant, and over time, the changes might be subtler. You need these people to become your advocate throughout the process, and it's important to communicate with them frequently so they feel emotionally connected to your innovation.

There will come a time when you'll need them to stand up and publicly endorse you, so courting them continuously is critical. These people will become your "lighthouse" customers that others will contact to validate your innovation's merit and value. You need these people to enthusiastically endorse not only the final iteration of the innovation, but also the process of collaboration.

Completing Map 6

1. **From your previous maps, you've probably got a good idea of whom you need to talk to.** Some are stressed people that you already know about. Others might be channel partners or vendors that directly affect you. From these, pick five or six people, list their name, organization, title, and the role they'll play in your innovation efforts.

2. **Develop a range of criteria to judge your potential allies.** Here are some potential criteria to think about:

   ▶ **Excited About Innovation.** Sees how your innovation solves a big problem or significantly accelerates growth

   ▶ **Shares Your Vision.** Believes your innovation conveys a picture of a desirable future

   ▶ **Sees Immediate Benefits.** Thinks your innovation promises realistic, attainable experiences with little investment or complexity

   ▶ **Has Peer Credibility.** Perceived as a leader, visionary, or smart operator

   ▶ **Willing To Publicly Endorse You.** Will go "on the record" supporting your innovation as a co-collaborator

3. **Now measure each potential ally against the criteria you've selected.** Use the following rating scale:

    10   Enthusiastic Advocate
    9   Strongly Supportive
    8   Supportive
    7   Interested
    6   Will Help Out
    5   Probably Won't Resist
    4   Uninterested
    3   Mildly Negative
    2   Strongly Opposed
    1   Antagonistic Anti-Sponsor

4. **Repeat for the other allies.** When you are done rating each potential alley, sum up the scores. The highest scores indicate the people you should solicit to collaborate on your innovation.

5. **To add more flexibility to the process, you can give your criteria different weights.** For instance, you might give your most important criterion a value of 20 points, your second criterion a value of 10 points, and your third criterion a value of 5 points. Play around until you've properly represented the relative importance of each criterion. Once you've found the correct weights, follow the same process as set out in steps 3 and 4 above.

6. **Finally, check your gut.** Do these choices feel like the right ones?

Map 6: Allies

Potential Ally	1	2	3
Name:			
Organization:			
Title:			
Role:			
Excited about innovation			
Shares your vision			
Sees immediate benefits			
Has peer credibility			
Willing to publically endorse you			
total score:			

Potential Ally	4	5	6
Name:			
Organization:			
Title:			
Role:			
Excited about innovation			
Shares your vision			
Sees immediate benefits			
Has peer credibility			
Willing to publically endorse you			
total score:			

Getting Insights from Map 6

1. **Do you have some enthusiastic advocates?** You will need these people to guide you through the development of your innovation. They will be the people to give you unbiased feedback essential to understanding the value of your innovation.

2. **Do you have some people who probably won't resist or will help out?** These people are important because they will help you understand the critical elements of your innovation that will drive adoption beyond your initial advocates.

3. **Do you have some people who are negative, opposed, or antagonistic?** It's okay to have one or two of these people because they will help you understand who won't adopt your innovation and why. Listen to what they have to say, but don't necessarily change your innovation to meet their demands, or you'll risk adding features and functionality that muddle your innovation efforts.

Debriefing Map 6

Capture what you've learned from this map by answering the following questions:

▶ What was most difficult about compiling your list of allies?

▶ What was most challenging about selecting the criteria?

▶ Was there any conflict doing this map? What was at the heart of the conflict?

MAP 7

VALUE PROPOSITION
Why Change?

Faced with the choice between changing one's mind and proving that there is no need to do so, almost everyone gets busy on the proof. — *John Kenneth Galbraith, Economist*

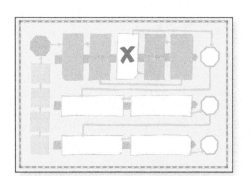

Visualization is a powerful human ability to imagine a future scenario. In sports, athletes imagine winning a championship and start to create images of success and test the route to their particular summit. What works for world-class athletes can work for you just as well.

One way to visualize why customers should change their behavior and adopt your innovation is to put customers into a story and then imagine where they will end up. This allows you to set the context of the story, create the characters, and set up your innovation as the hero.

Story Structure

The simplest way for telling a story is the three-frame cartoon strip. In that strip, you have the three basic components of the story:

ONCE UPON A TIME... where you set things up and introduce your prospective customer...

SUDDENLY... things shift, the challenge becomes clear...

AND THEN... resolution! Your innovation changes how things work out in the end.

By telling a story, you can test possible innovation scenarios. Storytelling is a way to visualize the future so you can make it more concrete. Playing out a scenario in story form can also enable you to see potential challenges, so you can adjust for them along the way.

Storytelling is key to great brands. Every great brand has a clear definition of its customers and prospects, their needs and desires, and how the brand delivers. When this structure is creatively executed (e.g., Coca-Cola, Disney, UPS), you create lasting impressions that increase customer affinity and loyalty.

Completing Map 7

1. **Bring to mind your innovation.** You're going to imagine how it is going to play out, and you're going to tell three variants of the story. You can either write down the story in the three-box structure of the map, or if you're so inclined, you can draw it in cartoon style.

2. **Your first story is the one in which things work out perfectly for your customer.** Everything falls into place. Everything you need shows up when you need it. You make all the right choices, and there's a happy ending. Tell that story in as much detail as you can, really imagining step-by-step how you arrive at the best possible outcome for your customer. It may be helpful to keeping asking, "And what happened next?" Resist the temptation to fast-forward to the ending without imagining the journey on the way. By describing the steps to success, you may generate even more good, new story ideas.

3. **Now tell a different story about the same challenge.** This time, imagine what happens if it doesn't go at all as planned: all sorts of unexpected challenges get thrown in your way, you're continually thwarted, and it's nothing but a struggle. And the ending—not so great. This will help reveal new elements you need to consider: fears, doubts, or uncertainty you may not have articulated.

4. **The final variation is in the middle.** It's neither great nor terrible, just a typical experience. How does that story unfold? Again, fill in as much detail as you can. This will help you understand the motivations of your customer in a typical transaction and identify if your innovation is compelling enough to cause them to change ingrained behaviors.

Map 7: Value Proposition

Once upon a time...

Our prospective customer is a (role)...

who wants to (job to be done)...

SUDDENLY...

she finds that (obstacles)...

so she must (compensating behaviors)...

And then...

She discovers (your capabilities)...

so she can now (benefits)...

Getting Insights from Map 7

1. **As you review your best-case story, look for the key choices you need to make.** Look for the moments of truth that will make or break your innovation.

2. **As you review your worst-case story, look for the things that might derail you.** Look for where the challenges lie and how things might unravel. This will help you avoid these pitfalls.

3. **Look at your final story and think about the regret and disappointment you'll feel if you don't take risks.**
Identify the places where playing it safe will result in incremental improvement and not true innovation.

Debriefing Map 7

Capture what you've learned from this map by answering the following questions:

▸ Which of these three stories was easiest to imagine? Which felt the most real?

▸ What do you now see as most critical for the success of your innovation?

▸ What concerns you?

▸ To be successful, what does the hero (your innovation) need to do? What does the hero need to avoid?

How do we know customers will buy this?

We collaborated with our customers to ensure we're creating value worth paying for.

YOUR DESIGN BRIEF

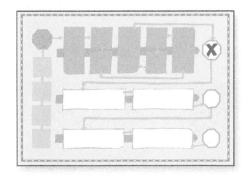

Good design accelerates the adoption of new ideas.
— Yves Béhar, Industrial Designer

Establishing your Design Brief is a critical step in creating your innovation. Your Design Brief should reflect who, what, where, when and how your innovation will work.

This information is critical to the innovation team members tasked with building prototypes or a Minimum Viable Product (MVP) for feedback. The Design Brief will set the general direction of what functionality is needed and will establish guidelines that the engineers, developers, and other creative members must follow.

When well written, your Design Brief will create the acceptance criteria for your innovation. Your Design Brief should describe the ideal qualities or attributes of a great solution, but not the solution itself.

Completing Your Design Brief

1. **Take out your Desirability Maps.**
   Review all of the maps to make sure they are updated with the most current information.

2. **Cut & Paste sections from your Desirability Maps.**
   Map 1: Stress
   Articulate the greatest stress(es) affecting prospective customers today.
   Map 2: Customer Experience
   Capture what specifically is creating stress(es) today.
   Map 3: Compensating Behaviors
   Identify the three lowest emotional points (and Compensating Behaviors, if any) in the current Customer Experience.
   Map 4: Solutions
   Explain your most promising ideas.
   Map 5: Assumptions
   State the key things you must validate or disprove.
   Map 6: Allies
   List the people who can provide feedback and collaborate on the design.
   Map 7: Value Proposition
   Describe your three-box cartoon or story.

3. **Look for consistency across the Design Brief.**
   What themes or trends or dynamics do you see? Do you have language that reflects the insights you've discovered? Is that language on your Design Brief?

Milestone 2: Design Brief

Stress	What stresses (behavioral, emotional) must the design alleviate? (Enter your results from Map 1)
Customer Experience	What specific steps (behavioral, emotional) create stresses today? (Enter your results from Map 2)
Compensating Behaviors	What are the three lowest emotional points and compensating behaviors (if any) in your Customer Experience? (Enter your results from Map 3)
Solutions	What are the most promising ideas to alleviate the stresses? (Enter your results from Map 4)
Assumptions	What assumptions must be validated or disproved? (Enter your results from Map 5)
Allies	Who can provide feedback and collaborate on the design? (Enter your results from Map 6)
Value Proposition	What must be offered to drive adoption of your innovation? (Enter your results from Map 7)

STAGE 2

FEASIBILITY

MAP 8 — **ASSETS:** What Assets Do You Have?

MAP 9 — **MINIMUM VIABLE PRODUCT:** What Can You Build?

MAP 8

ASSETS
What Assets Do You Have?

Do not wait; the time will never be 'just right.' Start where you stand, and work with whatever tools you may have at your command. — *George Herbert, Welsh Poet*

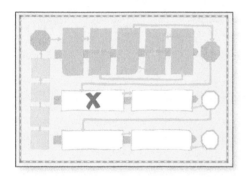

No innovation effort ever has enough resources. There is never enough time or money to do what you think is necessary. But this is rarely the reason innovation efforts fail to match up to your vision. The inability to produce a working prototype comes not from a lack of resources, but a lack of creativity.

The engineers of the Apollo 13 space mission are a great example of how to work with limited resources to create not just a prototype, but also a life-saving innovation. As you may recall, the in-flight accident of Apollo 13 caused a carbon dioxide filter to malfunction. Without the filter, the astronauts would die from CO_2 poisoning.

The engineers on the ground had to find a way to use the assets onboard the crippled spacecraft to create a solution. In the end, the engineers used a combination of duct tape, a cardboard notebook, and plastic moon rock bags to build a prototype on the ground that they tested in a simulator. They built a series of rapid prototypes until they validated or refuted their assumptions. Armed with these insights, they instructed the astronauts how to build a CO_2 filter that dropped the cabin pressure from a deadly 15 millimeters to a safe .2 millimeters and saved their lives.

Overlooked, Existing, and Untried Assets

This map will focus on asking, "What can we use to build something?" Many organizations feel shackled because resources are so scarce, but there are usually several options available to build incredible prototypes and MVPs.

Start with the assets you have on your innovation team. People are the most precious assets and are often underutilized. What unique skills do people have that might be overlooked because these skills are not in their formal job description?

Next, look at the existing business processes you have in place. You probably have several such as daily scrums, weekly team meetings, product backlogs, or senior executive reviews. Maybe you have burn rates, status reports, or project management systems.

Perhaps you have access to emerging technology like 3D printing, or you might be skilled in software that instantly turns your designs into clickable prototypes while presenting them in their native operating environment. Maybe you've used tools that transform PowerPoint and Keynote presentations into functioning mobile, tablet, or desktop applications. These capabilities are readily available for a nominal investment of a few hundred dollars and some software applications even offer free trials.

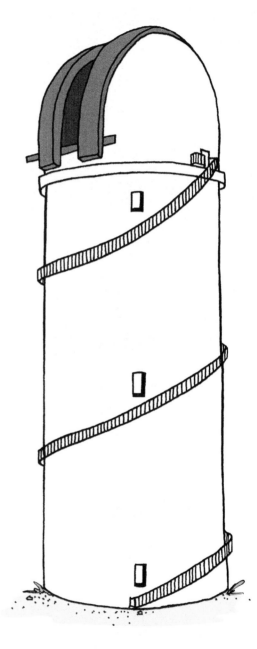

Completing Map 8

1. **Start at the top of the map with, "What assets do you already have?"** This allows you to jot down your current thoughts about how you might build your MVP. These assets might be big and powerful or small and detailed. Write them all down. Keep going until you run out of assets.

2. **Now you're ready for some different approaches.** Scan the remaining questions and pick one that you like. Use it to generate another 15 assets in 5 minutes.

3. **Pick a second question and do the same thing.** Generate another 15 assets in 5 minutes.

4. **Continue the process until you've answered all the questions.** Be sure to generate 15 assets in 5 minutes for each question.

5. **Now draw a "magnifying glass" next to the assets that you need to look into more deeply.** You may be unfamiliar with the asset, you may be missing some critical information, or you may need to find someone with a certain skillset who isn't currently on your innovation team.

Map 8: Assets

What assets do you already have in your organization?

What assets have other industries used?

What assets worked in previous innovations?

What assets do you need to move quickly?

What assets have you always wanted to work with?

What new technology assets can you try?

Getting Insights from Map 8

1. **Review all the assets you've written down.** Pay attention to the ones that you gravitate toward. Why do you like them? Are they safe and predictable? If so, then write down the ones that make you feel less safe and predictable.

2. **Review the assets that are new to you.** How can these new technologies produce rapid prototypes faster, cheaper, or better? What does that say to you?

Debriefing Map 8

Let the lessons of the map sink in by answering these questions:

▸ What was it like to list the assets you already had? Did you have more or fewer assets than you thought?

▸ Which were your favorite new questions? What does that say to you?

▸ Was this process difficult or easy for you? Why do you think you felt this way?

▸ Did you notice a tendency to evaluate the assets as they were created? What is that saying about your willingness to try new assets that could produce rapid prototypes?

MAP 9

MINIMUM VIABLE PRODUCT
What Can You Build?

The true method of knowledge is experimentation.
— William Blake, 18th Century Visual Artist

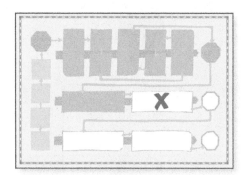

Your MVP is your first attempt to deliver value to your customer. Since you already understand why stresses occur, developed ideas to alleviate those stresses, and even collected the assets to build your solution, it's now time to stop talking and start building.

To guide you, here is the working definition of MVP that Brant Cooper and Patrick Vlaskovits use in their book, *The Lean Entrepreneur.* They explain, "a minimum viable product must be comprised of the least amount of functionality necessary to solve a problem sufficiently such that your customer will engage with your innovation and even pay you for it."

Building an MVP will take more than one try. You're not going to nail it the first time out. Think about the process of writing a proposal or a presentation. How many times do you edit, cut and paste, modify, and rearrange until you have something that does the job?

The reality of today's rapid prototyping world is that you're never done, so you might as well get your innovation in the hands of some customers as soon as possible. You won't learn what you're missing or getting wrong until you let someone try to use it. That's why it's called a *Minimum* Viable Product.

Three Types of Buyers

When you are creating your MVP, you will be engaged in an iterative set of activities, done quickly, and aimed at transforming your ideas into something tangible. You need to give your ideas detail, form, and function so your customers can evaluate them rather than imagine them.

It's important to note that the first role of the MVP is to focus on what to build for whom. Your innovation is likely to impact three different types of buyers: Decision Maker, User, and Blocker. The Decision Maker authorizes spending money, the User consumes the product or service, and the Blocker decides if the product or service is "good enough."

For example, if you are introducing a new snack food for teenagers, you'll probably need to persuade parents to buy it, kids to eat it, and kid peers to think it's cool. If you are introducing a new business software product, you'll probably need to persuade managers to think it's worth the investment, users to find it is intuitive to use, and the IT department to decide it meets their performance criteria. Even if the three types of buyers are the same person (e.g., an individual buying a new mobile phone), you'll still need to demonstrate why it's worth buying, how it works, and how to maintain it.

TIPS & TRICKS

Building your MVP can be tricky, but it doesn't need to be. The important thing is to roll up your sleeves and build something! Early prototypes are usually crude and unfinished in appearance. They look like what they are—work in progress.

But this incompleteness actually helps you. It invites people to interact with and improve on the MVP. This collaboration will allow you to gain valuable insight on how to improve your innovation at a very low cost.

Just be sure to create enough functionality to persuade all three types of buyers that you're on the right track. This will open their minds to new possibilities and engage them in building the next prototype. By soliciting their input, you'll be inoculating your innovation from future objections.

Most important, don't worry about failure. One of the key problems in large organizations is that they avoid failure like the plague. Innovation teams too often play it safe to avoid "failure"—even if failure gives the organization tremendous insight or prevents the organization from wasting a lot of money.

Try instead to reframe the MVP challenge. You simply want to "find out if something is feasible or not." This will allow you to push the envelope and shut down any objections. After all, what's the harm in trying something innovative if all you're doing is assessing its "feasibility?"

Completing Map 9

1. **Describe your three different buyers in their respective boxes on the map.** Remember these definitions: The Decision Maker is the singular person who decides to spend money (or not), and asks, "What ROI will I get?" It could be a parent, a vice-president, or the head of a department.

   The User asks, "How will it work for me?" These are the people that you must serve and make their lives easier or better.

   The Blocker asks, "Does it meet specifications?" These people are too often ignored and, consequently, love to say no to change. Pay attention to them because they are the first people to raise objections about your innovation.

2. **List the minimum functionality for each type of buyer.** Focus on what each really needs, not what they may want. By focusing on what they need, you'll be able to avoid feature and function bloat. The rule of thumb for determining minimum functionality is "less is more."

3. **List the jobs that the minimum functionality will allow each type of buyer to do.** Each piece of functionality should directly link to a job that must be done. This linkage will explain why the functionality is critical.

4. **Finally, list the benefits each completed job will deliver.** You don't need to be particularly specific. You can categorize the benefits as doing something better, faster, cheaper, or easier.

Map 9: Minimum Viable Product

The Decision Maker

This person…

Needs this minimum functionality…

So they can do these jobs…

That will result in these benefits…

The User

This person…

Needs this minimum functionality…

So they can do these jobs…

That will result in these benefits…

The Blocker

This person…

Needs this minimum functionality…

So they can do these jobs…

That will result in these benefits…

Getting Insights from Map 9

1. **As you review your minimum functionality list, look for the key choices you need to make.** Look for the moments of truth that will make or break your innovation.

2. **As you review your jobs list, look for the things that might derail you.** Look for where the challenges lie and how things might unravel. This will help you avoid these pitfalls.

3. **Look at your benefits and review the Value Proposition you created in Map 7.** Identify where the benefits are aligned with your Value Proposition and where they are not in alignment. What does this say to you?

Debriefing Map 9

Capture what you've learned from this map by answering the
following questions:

▸ Which type of buyer was easiest to imagine? Which felt
the most real?

▸ What do you now see as most critical for the success
of your innovation?

▸ Where does danger lurk?

▸ Before you get feedback on your innovation, what absolutely,
positively must work?

YOUR FEEDBACK PLAN

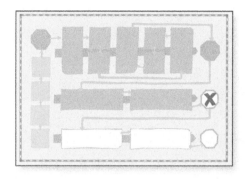

That's the reason they are called lessons, because they 'lessen' from day to day. **— Lewis Carroll, Author**

Congratulations! You've now built a MVP based on alleviating key stress points and have created what you think is a compelling Value Proposition that will cause people to willingly open their wallets and throw money at you.

Now you need to gather some feedback from the real world. The goal of getting feedback on your MVP is not to find out what's right with it, but rather what's wrong with it. At this point, you're not trying to see if you can "sell it." Instead, you're still trying to see how much you can learn.

Your MVP interviews should be with the Allies that you identified in Map 6. You should conduct your interviews in person so you can observe what they are doing and how they are doing it. You will want to compare the feedback you receive with your Design Brief.

To create your feedback plan, refer to Map 3 identifying the steps in the customer journey where the most acute stress occurs. Then sort these steps in the journey by the Buyer Types you listed in Map 9.

For example, suppose your innovation is a "one-stop-shop" web portal for third-party retailers to get everything they need to sell your product in their stores. The manufacturer CEO (Decision Maker) stress might be that retailers aren't currently implementing a new pricing strategy. The manufacturer CMO (User) stress might be that the retailers don't understand what they are supposed to do. The manufacturer CIO (Blocker) stress might be to limit access to the portal to a select group of authorized users so the new pricing plan won't fall into the wrong hands.

You'll need to collect feedback on how well each buyer type thinks your solution alleviates their pain. Then, invite them to tell you what's wrong with your solution. This will help them articulate what you may need to address in your next iteration. You don't need to follow their advice, but you do need to understand it.

Completing Your Feedback Plan

1. **Take out Maps 9, 6, and 3.**
   Review each map to make sure they are updated with the most current information.

2. **Look at Map 9: MVP.**
   Cut and paste the description of each buyer type into the first column of your Feedback Plan.

3. **Look at Map 6: Allies.**
   Cut and paste the appropriate names into the first column of your Feedback Plan. The descriptions from Map 9 and the names from Map 6 should be compatible.

4. **Look at Map 3: Compensating Behaviors.**
   Cut and paste the emotional low points and emotion levels into the corresponding columns of your Feedback Plan.

5. **Go out into the market and talk to your Allies.**
   You only need to ask them two questions:
   #1. How does this solution make things better for you?
   #2. What's wrong with the solution?
   Their answers will give you enough information to build the next iteration of your solution prototype.

Milestone 3: Feedback Plan

Decision Maker	Stressful Step	Emotion Level	How does this solution make things better for you?	What's wrong with the solution?
Description from Map 9 Allies from Map 6	From Map 3	From Map 3		

User	Stressful Step	Emotion Level	How does this solution make things better for you?	What's wrong with the solution?
Description from Map 9 Allies from Map 6	From Map 3	From Map 3		

Blocker	Stressful Step	Emotion Level	How does this solution make things better for you?	What's wrong with the solution?
Description from Map 9 Allies from Map 6	From Map 3	From Map 3		

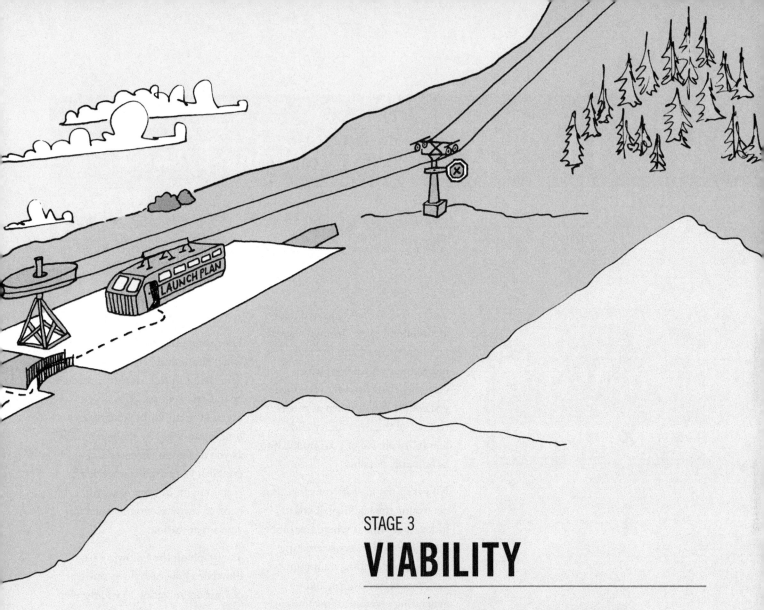

STAGE 3

VIABILITY

MAP 10

COST STRUCTURE
What's Your Break-Even?

Pearls don't lie on the seashore. If you want one, you must dive for it.
— Chinese proverb

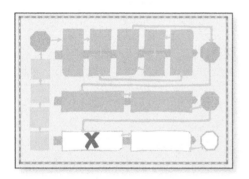

You've done it. You've tested your assumptions, gone through several rapid prototypes, and learned more about your prospective customer than you ever imagined you could. You've taken as much risk out of the desirability and feasibility phases of your innovation as humanly possible.

Now it's time to shift your focus to determine the viability of your innovation. This is where the rubber meets the road, because creating and delivering value, maintaining customer relationships, and generating revenue all involve costs to your organization.

Fortunately, there is one simple test to see if your innovation is viable for your organization. It is determining your break-even point, i.e., the revenue (or unit) sales needed to equal your expense rate.

Three-Year Timeframe

Every organization needs to know when an innovation will start generating a profit or start to reduce operating expenses. This is your break-even point. In general, an innovation will lose money initially as you incur startup costs and establish your fixed costs, but at a certain point in time, you will need to create economic value for your organization.

The graph on the following page illustrates how cash flows out of your organization as you develop your innovation and prepare to launch it. These costs are inevitable, and they represent your organization's financial risk. Over time, your sales will generate more and more profit until you reach your break-even point. Every sale beyond the break-even point will generate value for your organization.

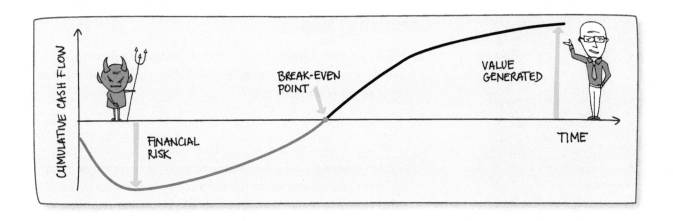

Many organizations seek to minimize their financial risk or "innovate on the cheap." There are a number of ways to keep your initial costs in check; however, you don't want to under-capitalize your innovation and jeopardize your initial sales goals or create unhappy customers due to poor product or service support.

You can calculate your break-even point over any timeframe, but according to *Harvard Business Review*, an organization's ability to project sales drops precipitously beyond a three-year horizon. Their research shows new competition, changing prices, different delivery systems, and other marketplace dynamics change too frequently to project much further into the future.

And since you don't want to invite doubt among senior executives or investors, your analysis should be limited to a timeframe that reasonable people can debate. Besides, if your innovation does not break-even and start generating value in three years, the likelihood of receiving additional investments is low, and it's better to just walk away. (Highly regulated industries, e.g., pharmaceutical and biotechnology, are the rare exceptions to this rule.)

Types of Costs

To calculate your break-even point, you'll need to consider three different types of cost.

Startup Costs

Costs that occur once before you can launch your innovation, e.g., engineering, product development, consulting, manufacturing tooling, distribution set-up, sales and marketing materials, legal expenses.

Run-The-Business (RTB) Fixed Costs

Costs that remain the same regardless of the amount of goods or services produced, e.g., salaries, rent, manufacturing facilities.

Run-The-Business (RTB) Variable Costs

Costs that vary depending on the amount of goods or services produced, e.g., time and materials used to create one unit of a good or service.

Completing Map 10

1. **Begin with your startup costs.** You should have a pretty good handle on these costs since you've probably engaged a number of firms to get you to this point.

2. **Now move on to your fixed costs for Year 1, Year 2, and Year 3.** Start estimating your minimum fixed costs to support and ramp up Year 1. Then move on to the fixed costs for the second year and third year. Year 2 and Year 3 costs should be greater than Year 1, but only marginally higher since you're likely to add only a few incremental people to your sales, marketing, and support teams.

3. **Next calculate your variable costs per unit.** This calculation is simply how much it costs you to produce a single unit. In a manufacturing company, this is the cost of goods sold. In a services company, this is more likely to be costs for people delivering the service.

4. **Now you're ready for some math.** To find out how many units you must sell to reach your break-even point, add your Startup Costs and your RTB Fixed Costs for Year 1, Year 2, and Year 3. Then, divide this number by the difference between your Unit Price and your Unit Cost. What you're doing is dividing all of your costs in the first three years by the gross margin contribution of each unit.

5. **Now calculate your break-even point in revenue.** Use the sum of Startup Costs and RTB Fixed Costs for Year 1, Year 2 and Year 3 that you calculated in Step 4. But this time, divide the sum by 1 minus your Unit Cost divided by your Unit Price. Now, you're dividing all of your costs in the first three years by the percentage of gross margin contribution of each unit.

Map 10: Cost Structure

Startup Costs:	Year 1
Engineering Fees	$_____
Developer Fees	$_____
Consultant Fees	$_____
Agency Fees	$_____
Legal Fees	$_____
Other	$_____
	$_____
	$_____
	$_____
Total	$_____

RTB Fixed Costs:	Year 1	Year 2	Year 3
Marketing Salaries	$_____	$_____	$_____
Sales Salaries	$_____	$_____	$_____
Customer Support Salaries	$_____	$_____	$_____
Product Support Salaries	$_____	$_____	$_____
Marketing Programs	$_____	$_____	$_____
Training Programs	$_____	$_____	$_____
General & Admin.	$_____	$_____	$_____
Other	$_____	$_____	$_____
	$_____	$_____	$_____
Annual Total	$_____	$_____	$_____
Three-Year Total			$_____

Break-even (Units) =

$$\frac{\text{Startup Costs + RTB Fixed Costs}}{\text{(Unit Price} - \text{Cost of Goods Sold Per Unit)}}$$

Break-even (Revenue) =

$$\frac{\text{Startup Costs + RTB Fixed Costs}}{1 - \text{(Cost of Goods Sold Per Unit/Unit Price)}}$$

RTB Variable Costs:	Year 1	Year 2	Year 3
Unit Average Cost	$_____	$_____	$_____

Getting Insights from Map 10

1. **Review all the costs you've written down.** How accurate do you think they are? Which costs do you lack confidence in? What can you do to increase your confidence?

2. **Review the costs that seem high to you.** How can you re-imagine the process using new technologies to reduce costs? What existing systems or processes can you leverage to lower costs and gain efficiencies?

Debriefing Map 10

Let the lessons of the map sink in by answering these questions:

▸ What did it feel like to list all of your costs? Did it make you feel nervous? Or did it make you feel eager to launch your innovation?

▸ How confident are you about achieving your break-even point? What do you think is going to be critical to your success?

▸ What's the probability of you achieving your break-even? 100%? 75%? 50%? Less?

When will you break-even?

We modeled our costs over a three-year time frame and expect to break-even in year "x."

MAP 11

LAUNCH PLAN
How Will You Go To Market?

The most anxious time was during launch, just because that is so dramatic. — *Sally Ride, U.S. Astronaut*

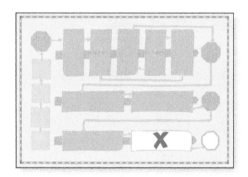

Now the fun starts. This is where you create your plans to take your innovation to market. It's where all the maps have led you. You're at the crest of going from idea to reality.

A lot of innovation, sales, and marketing books add layers of complexity to this process. But all innovation follows the same adoption curve. It starts with people who thoroughly embrace innovation, quickly shifts to early adopters who like new things but don't want to be on the cutting edge, and then slowly migrates to the early majority or mainstream.

Most people readily understand this adoption curve. But they often fail to appreciate the distinct differences of each group and ignore the fact that they require different value propositions. Geoffrey A. Moore made this insight famous in his book, *Crossing the Chasm: Marketing and Selling High-Tech Products to Mainstream Customers.*

Moore explained the importance of focusing on one group of customers at a time, using each group as a credible reference to market to the next group. He demonstrated that the most difficult step is making the transition from the visionaries (innovators and early adopters) to the pragmatists (early majority or mainstream). This is the chasm he refers to and crossing that chasm is critical to accelerate adoption of your innovation and make it an unqualified success.

Visionaries
SPIRITED FREE ORIGINAL abstract LOVE innovation NEW Quest INTUITIVE BROAD

PRAGMATISTS
EXHAUSTIVE ANALYSIS
MULTIPLE OPTIONS
BEST CHOICE
DEFENSIBLE RATIONALE
ABHORS RISK
SLOW TO DECIDE

Differences Between Visionaries and Pragmatists

Visionaries are eager to try out innovations. They appreciate an innovation's potential to make life better, cheaper or easier. They want to be seen as progressive people leading others to try new ideas and approaches. Because this is their natural disposition, they are often more than willing to give your innovation their endorsement and act as an active reference for you.

Fortunately, communicating with visionaries is easier than ever before. Social media, community and enthusiast forums, blogs, and other media make gaining access to these opinion leaders relatively easy and inexpensive.

Pragmatists are much more traditional. They tend to buy innovations after they get solid references from sources they trust (e.g., Consumer Reports) and become convinced an innovation will not fail for them. What makes these people challenging is that they frequently see themselves as innovators. They are often interested in innovation and may even be responsible for discovering innovation for their organization, but their actual behavior does not match their idealized self-perception.

These differences require you to change your Value Proposition over time. For example, the visionaries who first purchased the Nissan LEAF 100% electric vehicle bought the car to help save the environment. They were concerned about global warming, reducing their carbon footprint, and believed that buying a Nissan LEAF was helping lead the U.S. toward a new energy policy.

But the pragmatists in the marketplace were quite different. While they liked the environmental benefits of the Nissan LEAF, they were much more concerned with how much they could save by going electric and bypassing the gasoline pump. They also wanted to know where they could plug in around town, how much they'd save in tax credits, and the residual value of the car when they traded it in or sold it to someone else.

The illustration above shows the different ways that visionaries and pragmatists buy products and services.

Completing Map 11

1. **Take out Map 9: MVP.** Review the map to make sure it is updated with the most current information.

2. **List the relevant message for Innovators.** Most Innovators are like the "Decision Maker" buyer type that you identified in Map 9 so cut and paste the minimum functionality, jobs to be done, and resulting benefits into the left-hand column under "What's Your Message?"

3. **Now list the relevant message for Early Adopters.** Most Early Adopters are like the "User" buyer type that you identified in Map 9 so cut and paste the minimum functionality, jobs to be done, and resulting benefits into the middle column under "What's Your Message?"

4. **Next, list the relevant message for Early Majority.** Most Early Majority adopters are like the "Blocker" buyer type that you identified in Map 9 so cut and paste the minimum functionality, jobs to be done, and resulting benefits into the right-hand column under "What's Your Message?"

5. **Finally, list the number of units you must sell to each customer segment.** You calculated your break-even point in Map 10. Use this information to determine how many units you must sell in Year 1, Year 2, and Year 3.

Map 11: Launch Plan

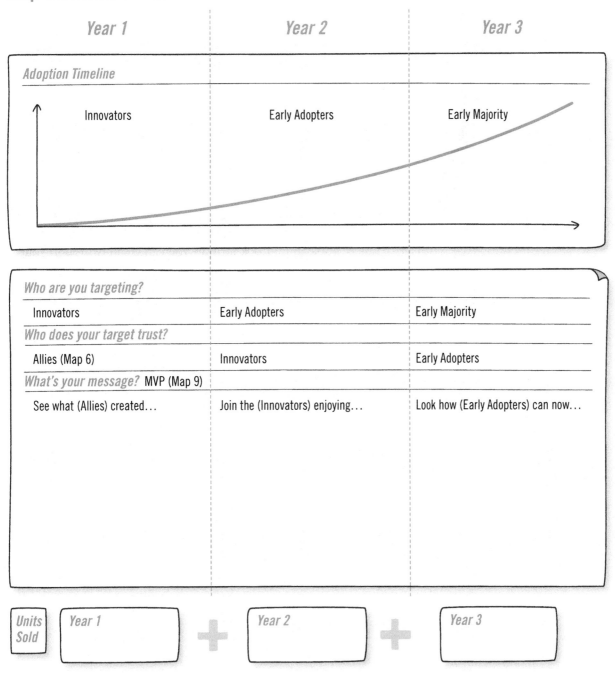

	Year 1	Year 2	Year 3

Adoption Timeline

Innovators   Early Adopters   Early Majority

Who are you targeting?

Innovators	Early Adopters	Early Majority

Who does your target trust?

Allies (Map 6)	Innovators	Early Adopters

What's your message? MVP (Map 9)

See what (Allies) created...	Join the (Innovators) enjoying...	Look how (Early Adopters) can now...

Units Sold

Year 1	➕	Year 2	➕	Year 3

Getting Insights from Map 11

1. **As you review your launch plan, look for the key promises you must deliver on.** Identify the moments of truth that will make or break your launch plan.

2. **As you review your messages, look for the things that might not be believable.** Look for how you can credibly support your claims.

3. **Look at your units sold.** Identify how likely you are to achieve this goal. What does this say to you?

Debriefing Map 11

Capture what you've learned from this map by answering the following questions:

▸ Which of these customer segments do you think will be most willing to adopt your innovation? Why?

▸ What do you now see as most critical for the adoption of your innovation?

▸ Where is there danger?

▸ To minimize the danger, what absolutely, positively must you do?

How are you going to launch this solution?

We'll target visionaries enthusiastic about innovation and use them as a reference for the pragmatists and mainstream.

OVERCOMING OBJECTIONS

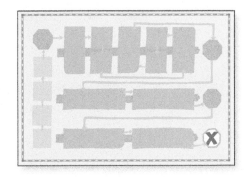

Intelligence is the ability to adapt to change.
— Steven Hawking, Theoretical Cosmologist

Your idea is now a reality. Admirers see you as a visionary. Peers yearn for your confidence and conviction. Management has its collective eyes on you. But be careful. The Devil's Advocate lies in wait for you.

Tom Kelley, founder of IDEO and author of *The Ten Faces Of Innovation*, has launched thousands of innovations, and he's seen the Devil's Advocate lurking around everywhere. Tom writes that the Devil's Advocate is always the person (or people) who assumes the most negative possible perspective to quash innovation. They represent a subtle, yet toxic, danger to your organization's cause, greatly diminishing the chance for innovation with negativity and naysaying.

So what can you do? In *The Art of The Start*, Guy Kawasaki suggests you "Make Mantra." He describes mantra as the act of making a sacred verbal vow with mystical potentialities. Guy believes the beauty of mantra is that everyone expects it to be short and sweet—and, therefore, understandable.

A Devil's Advocate hates mantra. You see, one of the most effective weapons of a Devil's Advocate is obfuscation—making communication confusing, purposefully ambiguous, and hard to interpret. When a Devil's Advocate obfuscates, it becomes difficult for people to make decisions. And if people can't make decisions, then nothing will change.

How To Overcome Objections

1. **Set up a one-hour meeting with your entire Innovation Team.** Overcoming Objections takes a team effort with each team member understanding and confidently playing their role when it's time to get a "Go/No Go" decision from senior management, investors, or other key stakeholders. The only way to properly prepare for this decision making process is to practice.

2. **At your practice meeting, divide the group into two teams.** One team will play the Devil's Advocate (DA) and the other will represent the role they played on the Innovation Team.

3. **Set a time limit of 3 minutes for each interaction** between the DA and the corresponding Innovation Team member. Let the conversation flow between the two participants uninterrupted. For example, the DA will ask, "How do we even know these are customer stresses?" The Product Owner will respond, "Like anthropologists, we observed customers in their environment." The DA could follow up with, "What exactly did you do?" The Product Owner could expand her response with fact-based information by adding, "We visited "x" number of customers in "y" geographies and spent "z" hours interviewing and observing real-world experiences." If the DA continues his objections, the Product Owner could utilize his mantra by saying, "We used Customer Centered Design. This means we put the Customer first. Is this something you object to?"

4. **At the end of each interaction, provide feedback from other team members.** Limit the feedback to 2 minutes. Focus on simplifying each team member's answers. Remember the DA likes to create obfuscation so fight back with clear, precise responses.

5. **Continue this process until each team member practices facing objections.** There are 11 team roles so if you keep to your time limits, then your meeting should be around an hour long.

Milestone 4: Overcoming Objections

Devil's Advocate Objection	Your Response	Your Mantra
How do we even know these are customer stresses?	Like anthropologists, we observed customers in their environment.	Customer Centered Design
How do you know what's causing the stress?	We mapped the customer experience to identify the root causes of stress.	Journey Mapping
What makes you think these stresses are bothering customers?	We learned how our customers must compensate for our shortcomings.	Pain Is Proof Positive
How do you know this is the best solution?	We used "T-Shaped" thinking to look across industries and deep into operational details.	"T"-Shaped Thinking
How do you know your solution will work for everyone involved?	We tested each of our critical assumptions in the marketplace.	Trust, But Verify
Who do you have lined up to support this solution?	We collaborated with key opinion leaders (and channel partners).	Collaborate. Don't Dictate
How do we know customers will buy?	We collaborated with our customers to ensure we're creating value worth paying for.	Alleviate Stress
What did you spend on this?	We spent 90 days to produce multiple working prototypes vetted by customers.	Speed Matters
Why doesn't it have "x" feature?	We built a minimum viable product and we will add features when customers demand them.	Less Is More
When will you break-even?	We modeled our costs over a three-year timeframe and expect to break-even in Year "x."	Slow and Steady
How are you going to launch this solution?	We'll target visionaries enthusiastic about innovation and use them as a reference for the pragmatists or mainstream.	Crossing The Chasm

STAGE 4
REACHING THE SUMMIT

SPEED MATTERS

FROM IDEA TO REALITY

SPEED MATTERS

Great ideas originate in the muscles.

— *Thomas A. Edison, Inventor*

The IN-90 Framework puts some structure and predictability around an uncertain and unpredictable process. This framework has been battle-hardened and time-tested with some of the greatest innovators in the last thirty years.

But the totality of the IN-90 regimen is more than a framework for rapid prototyping and customer feedback. It's also about speed.

As I mentioned in the foreword, 90% of all innovation projects die after their 90th day of life. This is an unfortunate fact of life for even the smartest and best-run organizations. There are a myriad of causes of death, including organizational neglect, cowardice, and, more recently, what seems like executive attention deficit disorder.

Whatever the cause, it's clear that the inherent biorhythm of organizations requires you to innovate quickly. If you don't, you will most certainly lose resources, funding, and momentum. Speed truly does matter.

The Key to Speed

Historically, every innovation, software or otherwise, started with requirements gathering. The assumption was that a combination of internal and external stakeholders knew exactly what they needed and all you needed to do was ask them.

But how could these groups envision something better, faster, cheaper, or easier when internal stakeholders, e.g., product development, IT, or purchasing, don't observe, collaborate, and iterate innovation with customers? And how could external stakeholders, i.e., customers, imagine a new solution when they don't know how your organization designs, manufactures, packages, distributes, sells, services, and supports your products and services. It is an impossible task.

This problem is compounded by how most organizations try to build innovations. Even if your organization assumed that you had all of the requirements, innovation teams were asked to build one piece of their innovation at a time in order for it to be critically reviewed and inspected during a "stage gate."

If the innovation didn't pass through the "gate," then the innovation teams were forced to go back and rebuild what they'd done. The natural consequence of this process was that the innovation teams became less bold and more conservative with each stage gate review. To avoid "rework," innovation teams would simply push the review further and further into the future.

The stage gate process (a.k.a., waterfall process) produced something that looked like the illustrations in the right sidebar. After each gate, there still wasn't enough functionality to release the innovation. While individual parts were thoroughly completed, the overall innovation was insufficiently completed to relieve customer pain.

Consequently, innovation teams frequently failed to deliver on time or budget. To make matters worse, when the innovation was ready, the requirements had changed so drastically that adoption was horribly low and ROI projections never came close to being accurate.

Thus, the Agile Methodology was conceived. It was started by a handful of software engineers who recognized they'd never adequately understand the scope of the innovation; therefore, it would be better to fix time and budget parameters and let functionality be variable.

Gate 1
6 months

Gate 2
12 months

Gate 3
18 months

Gate 4
24 months

Gate 5
30 months

Rough Frame
2 weeks

Basic Functionality
4 weeks

MVP
8 weeks

Advanced
Functionality
10 weeks

Never
Completed

This approach (illustrated in the left sidebar) allowed them to rapidly prototype something that the innovation team could evaluate. It gave the team more opportunities to talk to customers and validate their assumptions. More important, the feedback loop allowed the team to build advanced functionality and nuances that would never have been previously known.

Although the Agile Methodology gained traction in the technology sector, it is not inherently technical, and you can easily adapt the tools and practices to other industries. The fundamentals of every innovation effort remain the same—you must produce something quickly so you can move on to the next iteration.

Each early iterative innovation effort will increase the business value you create by leaps and bounds. But there are diminishing returns on every innovation effort. In most cases, simply going one or two iterations beyond the initial MVP will adequately address the stresses of customers.

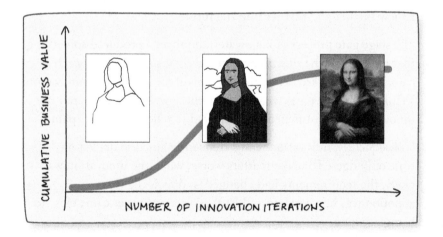

So it doesn't matter if you are coming up with the next great salty snack, creating social media content, manufacturing garage doors, or building next year's sales and marketing programs, you can use the Agile Methodology to create breakthrough innovations.

Agile Methodology Practices

Now you may be thinking that it's obvious there are diminishing returns on your innovation efforts. But think about many times you have poured hours and effort into ideas, programs, and initiatives to get them as close to perfect as possible. How many times should you have stopped earlier because you really needed feedback before going any further?

It takes a lot of courage to ask for help in an organization. That's why people have private conversations behind closed doors. They don't want anyone to think they need any help or feedback. Fortunately, the Agile Methodology has specific practices and tools to encourage collaboration and feedback.

Here are the critical tools:

Innovation Backlog
This is a cumulative list of maps necessary for your innovation. This includes all the elements of the Project Charter, Design Brief, Feedback Plan, and Launch Plan.

Sprint
The Sprint is the foundational rhythm of the Agile Methodology. It is a finite length of time, i.e. two weeks, where you bite off small pieces of your innovation and finish them before returning to bite off a few more. At the end of each Sprint, you must be ready to deliver a shippable product increment.

Sprint Backlog
This is the innovation team's 'to do' list for the Sprint. Unlike the Innovation Backlog, it has a finite lifespan, i.e., the length of the current Sprint.

The fundamentals of every innovation effort remain the same — you must produce something quickly so you can move on to the next iteration.

Shippable Product

At the end of each Sprint, the innovation team should produce a working prototype. It is not enough to produce wireframes or storyboards; you must convert these ideas to reality. The Executive Champion may choose not to ship what you've produced, but at the end of each Sprint you must assume it is your final Sprint.

Daily Scrum

The Daily Scrum requires participation of everyone on the innovation team and should be held at the start of each workday. Under no circumstances should the meeting last for more than 15 minutes. Each team member quickly shares three things:

1. Tasks completed since last scrum
2. Tasks expected to be completed by next scrum
3. Obstacles slowing me down

Task Board

The Task Board consists of three columns: To Do, Doing, Done. The board should be visible to everyone in the innovation room to provide all with complete visibility. It helps stakeholders see the progress the team is making and invites collaboration.

Obstacle Resolution

Every obstacle should be resolved by the next Daily Scrum. Any innovation team member can volunteer to address the obstacle, but they must commit to resolving it quickly. If an obstacle is not addressed after two Daily Scrums, it needs to be escalated to the Executive Champion.

Burn Chart

This chart shows the relationship between time (X-axis) and scope (Y-axis). The chart shows you what's left to do. Every time the scope increases, the line on the chart moves up, and when the scope decreases, the line on the chart moves down.

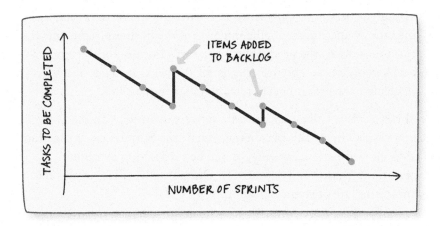

Sprint Reviews

The Sprint Review is the public end of a Sprint where all stakeholders are invited to review what the innovation team has accomplished. The innovation team will demonstrate what new insights, functionality, or benefits have been produced so the stakeholders can provide feedback.

Sprint Retrospective

A Sprint Retrospective is held at the end of every Sprint Review to focus on what was learned during the Sprint and how that learning can be applied to make process improvements. The goal is not to make a laundry list of things that went well or poorly, but to identify one or two changes to make in the next Sprint.

Agile Methodology Roles & Responsibilities

The Agile Methodology recognizes only three distinct roles and responsibilities:

Executive Champion

This is the person you identified in Map 4 who holds the vision for the innovation, represents the interests of the business, represents the customers, owns the product backlog, sets priorities for the product backlog, creates acceptance criteria for the backlog items, and is available to answer innovation team member questions.

The Executive Champion must be actively involved with the innovation effort. This person must chair the Sprint Review meeting with cross-functional colleagues and be prepared to overcome objections quickly and definitively. Quite simply, failure in this role ensures failure of your innovation.

Scrum Master

The Project Manager you identified in Map 4 will facilitate the Daily Scrum, act as a guide to team members, document product backlog and sprint backlog, track burn rate, and lead the Sprint Review.

The Scrum Master must be involved in coordinating, scheduling, documenting, and attending to the details on behalf of the innovation team. No one else is backing up the Scrum Master, so this person must be self-driven, highly motivated, and able to act with little or no supervision.

Team Members

These are the other members of the innovation team you identified in Map 4. They are responsible for completing assigned tasks, creating work estimates, participating in Daily Scrums and Sprint Reviews.

Team Members must be collaborators by nature. It's important that everyone carries their own load, but it's equally important that they are willing to lend a helping hand. Everyone gets stuck sometimes and needs some feedback or guidance. Each team member must be willing to step up when needed.

Agile and the Innovation Framework

It should come as no surprise to you that the Innovation Framework was designed with the Agile Methodology in mind. The table below shows how to translate the Desirability, Feasibility, and Viability stages into discrete two-week Sprints.

SPRINT #1: Desirability I
Sprint Backlog:

Project Charter
Map 1: Stress Map
Map 2: Customer Experience Map
Map 3: Compensating Behaviors Map

SPRINT #2: Desirability II
Sprint Backlog:

Map 4: Solutions Map
Map 5: Assumptions Map
Map 6: Allies Map
Map 7: Value Proposition Map

SPRINTS #3 & 4: Feasibility
Sprint Backlog:

Design Brief
Map 8: Assets Map
Map 9: MVP Map
Feedback Plan

SPRINTS #5 & 6: Viability
Sprint Backlog:

Map 10: Cost Structure
Map 11: Launch Plan
Overcoming Objections

To Be or Not to Be Agile

Some organizations already have in place an innovation, project management, or complex problem solving methodology like TQM, Six Sigma, or ISO 9001. In my experience, these process management programs kill innovation rather than encourage and support it.

In fact, Wharton Business School professor Mary Benner and Harvard Business School professor Michael Tushman write in *Exploitation, Exploration, and Process Management: The Productivity Dilemma Revisited* that most process management methodologies are only good for improving efficiency. Their research showed these tools are inappropriate for innovation, and they can actually drag organizations down and dampen innovation.

Today, organizations ranging from P&G to IBM to 3M acknowledge a renewed attention on gaining competitive advantage through innovation. Even GE, an early evangelist of Six Sigma, is using Agile Methodology for its innovation efforts. GE's internal research found that exploitation, i.e., searching for cost reductions and efficiencies, crowded out exploration of breakthrough innovation.

So try to make the case for using the Agile Methodology on one important innovation project. Position your efforts as a "pilot test." Then, you show everyone how you were able to take an idea to reality in 90 days. Once your organization sees how easy, collaborative, and fast the Agile Methodology is to use for innovation, you'll never go back.

FROM IDEA TO REALITY

The spread of innovation may be likened to a fire; first, a feeble spark, next a flickering flame, then a mighty blaze, ever increasing in speed and power.

— Nikola Tesla, Inventor

It's been said that it takes a village to raise a child. Well, it takes a team to commercialize an innovation. But too often team members turn on each other when adoption doesn't happen immediately.

So it's important for everyone to realize that adoption takes patience. It took the iPod over two years to sell one million units. Two years later, iPod sales were 10 million units. Two years after that, iPod sales were 20 million units. Everyone remembers the "overnight" success. No one remembers the first years of the iPod.

Expect change to come slowly, but steadily. Remember that the size of the Visionaries population is dwarfed by the size of the Pragmatist population. And remember that adoption is sequential, so you need to give your marketing team time to build demand, your sales team time to qualify and close, your product team time to deliver, and your product support team time to work through any problems with the complete ecosystem.

The Key to Commercialization

The key to successfully shifting from innovation to commercialization starts with understanding the four jobs to be done. Each job is discretely different, but often there is still confusion about who should do what. If these roles and responsibilities are not clarified early on, there is bound to be a lot of finger pointing and blame shifting.

Here's a simple way to organize who should do what:

The Marketing Job

Create Demand. That's all marketing should do. Now, the marketing business is replete with jargon. It's easy to get trapped in a marketing conversation loaded with phrases like "investing in awareness to maximize the buyer experience and increase brand relevancy." If you run into someone that uses these phrases, just walk away. You need each and every marketing activity to create demand for your innovation. That's it. Nothing more.

The Sales Job

Qualify and Close. That's all sales should do. Yes, Marketing is responsible for creating demand for your innovation, but no one has written a purchase order, signed a contract, or surrendered a credit card yet. The Sales team must to do this, and they will need to collaborate with Marketing to persuade customers to willingly adopt your innovation. This change in behavior cannot be coerced, forced, or mandated.

The Operations Job

Fulfill and Thrill. This is the most important part of commercialization. You may think the hardest part is getting a customer, but operations steps in when there is a problem. Usually customers are frustrated or, at least, worried about whether they've made a good decision, and the operations team must put their minds at ease.

The Customer Service Job

Love and Nurture. There will always be questions and problems that arise after the delivery of your innovation. You've asked customers to radically change their behavior and venture into the unknown. This is a scary time. Customer Service must demonstrate they genuinely care and want to help. Unfortunately, many organizations look at Customer Service as an expense, rather than an investment in brand loyalty.

KNOW WHERE YOU STAND

Meet every two weeks with each functional group. Ask each group to find out from your customers:

1) Would they recommend your innovation to others?

2) If yes, why? And, if not, why not?

These responses will unearth key innovation insights that you can use to continuously improve.

CASE STUDIES

SUCCESSFUL JOURNEYS

CASE STUDY 1 — **COCA-COLA FREESTYLE**

CASE STUDY 2 — **FRIENDS & FAMILY PLAN**

CASE STUDY 3 — **MOBILE DIGITAL MEDIA**

CASE STUDY
COCA-COLA FREESTYLE

Running a restaurant is a tough job. You open early and close late, usually seven days a week. You have to deal with staff, customers, and dozens of vendors. If just one thing goes wrong, you don't just run the risk of losing customers for the day, you may lose them for life.

This means everyone in the restaurant ecosystem must be focused on operational excellence. A restaurant needs three things from a vendor: high quality products, an efficient distribution system, and highly reliable equipment and service.

The Coca-Cola Company enjoyed a dominant market share of the restaurant industry, but it wanted to understand how to protect and grow the business. So teams of Coca-Cola employees went into the marketplace and conducted interviews, ethnographies, and even worked in restaurants serving beverages so they could experience first-hand what their customers experienced every day.

What they learned surprised them. Customers complained about lifting, moving, and storing the heavy five-gallon boxes of Coca-Cola syrup needed to produce a beverage. They also didn't like that they needed to inspect and (if necessary) repair the dispensing system every day to make sure the beverages tasted right. They were frustrated that they never knew for sure when they might run out of syrup because they didn't know which beverages were being sold most often. Finally, they felt like the response time to get service was too long (even though a service agent was often at the restaurant in less than four hours).

Coca-Cola had business and operational concerns as well. They had a fragmented distribution system that was expensive to maintain. Moreover, the distribution system didn't track inventory very accurately so customers were slow to pay until the invoices

were reconciled with delivery receipts. This was a labor-intensive process to manage and often put Coca-Cola in a reactive position rather than the proactive position of a committed partner.

There were some shared concerns of both customers and Coca-Cola. Both wanted to expand the number of beverages available in the restaurant. Both wanted to serve a high quality beverage. And both wanted to make sure the restaurant was never out-of-stock of Coca-Cola products.

One customer provided this compelling insight, "You guys at Coca-Cola have trained us over the years to think of a soft drink dispenser as a cash machine—as long as it's flowing, then I'm making money. So I want to be always fully stocked, always fully operational, and always delivering a high-quality product. Do that, and I'll be a customer for life!"

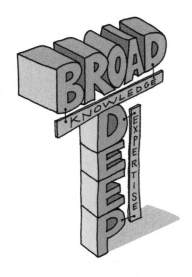

Now the problem had been reframed: Rather than make incremental improvements to existing processes, Coca-Cola had to innovate a completely new ecosystem. So a group of cross-functional Coca-Cola employees met to envision solutions to their complex problem. They started the process by reviewing ideas they already had conceived.

For example, one idea was to increase the size of the syrup package. This seemed counter-intuitive, but it could solve some out-of-stock problems and reduce delivery costs. This was an existing idea and the innovation team started to stretch their thinking.

One person observed that both Coca-Cola and UPS of "We Love Logistics" fame had their headquarters in Atlanta. So the team decided to sit down with UPS and collaborate on how UPS could solve some of product delivery and tracking issues facing Coca-Cola. This was the most efficient solution to pursue.

To improve beverage quality, Coca-Cola considered sending out service agents once every ninety days to do proactive service on every customer's dispensing system. This solution leveraged an existing infrastructure and required no additional training. This was the easiest solution to pursue.

But the team struggled to find a comprehensive solution to the multi-dimensional problem they faced. This is when they turned to their outside agencies and consultants for some new thinking. They needed some "T-shaped thinkers" with broad industry knowledge and deep technical expertise.

These T-shaped thinkers brought a much-needed fresh perspective. While engaged in an exercise creating analogies, one of the T-shaped thinkers thought about how ink jet printers use cartridges to create a rainbow of colors. Could this same approach be used to create a wide variety of beverages?

For example, could the same two cartridges used to make lemon-lime Sprite be used to put lemon in Minute Maid lemonade or put lime flavor in Coca-Cola classic? If this were true, then wouldn't that mean dozens of beverages could be created with only a few cartridges? This was clearly a provocative and industry-leading solution to pursue.

But there were a number of assumptions involved in this solution. Could the syrup be more concentrated? The syrup was already concentrated, but how much more concentrated could it be? What was the minimum number of cartridges required to create the maximum number of beverages?

Could the team bundle together some other ideas to make this solution even stronger? For example, could the dispensing system automatically reorder when a cartridge was running low of concentrate? Could the new dispensing system test itself like a printer conducts its own diagnostics?

Rather than try to answer all of the assumptions all at once, and risk scope creep and feature bloat, the innovation team boiled down the assumptions to three core questions: Can we produce syrup cartridges? Can we build a self-monitoring machine? What impact will we have on restaurant operations?

Now it was time to identify who could answer these questions. Because the assumptions were so clearly defined, it was obvious that the innovation team needed help from three very different sets of experts.

First, the innovation team needed to meet with their internal product development chemists. They needed to explore the "art of the possible" challenging the status quo. (This is where the desktop printer analogy paid huge dividends. The chemists quickly and easily understood what was being asked of them.)

Next, the innovation team met with the equipment manufacturers. Fortunately, there were two large manufacturers with Research and Development teams already in place. These R&D teams shared what they were working on and the innovation team gathered even more ideas on how the equipment might perform.

Finally, the innovation team needed to identify customers that would be willing to provide feedback on the design, installation, and ongoing maintenance of the entire new ecosystem. Since there was some risk of equipment failure using prototypes, the team decided to look for a customer that could install several machines in one location for redundancy purposes. The ideal testing ground: movie theaters.

But before the innovation team could approach movie theater customers, they needed to clarify and define their Value Proposition. They decided to draw a simple three-frame cartoon strip.

In the first frame, they set up the situation by acknowledging that serving a variety of high quality beverages can be really hard. The innovation team felt that they needed to clearly demonstrate empathy with the challenges of being a restaurant owner.

In the second frame, they imagined a "genie" that could make the operation hassles go away. They didn't explain exactly how this would work only that inventory, ordering, quality assurance, and equipment servicing would happen automatically.

In the third frame, also known as the "payoff" frame, the dispenser produced a string of o's and 1's (representing Internet connectivity) and a menu of dozens of delicious beverage options. Next to the dispenser stood a beaming restaurant owner with dollars spilling out of his pockets.

It's important to note that this cartoon took the perspective of the customer, not The Coca-Cola Company. There are obviously a lot of benefits that will accrue to the company, but customers don't care about those benefits. A customer only wants to know "what's in it for me?"

Too often organizations focus internally on the problem, solution, and payoff. This is the wrong approach. As George Day and Christine Moorman wrote in *Strategy From The Outside In*, it's only when you view things from the "Outside" that you'll uncover where you can create value "Inside."

But you can fall into the "Outside In" trap anywhere along your innovation journey. The Coca-Cola innovation team fell into the trap when they generated their list of assets. They first thought of all of their internal departments that could help, e.g., Product Development, Manufacturing, Service, and Marketing.

The problem with an innovation team composed of just internal departments is multi-faceted. First, if the departments are running efficiently and effectively, then there is no excess capacity of time, people, or money. Second, the best and brightest people in each organization will likely be assigned critical projects for the department, so you'll be missing out on the most capable people. Finally, this internal focus ensures that you'll narrow your thinking on what solutions might work because everyone will be trying to protect his "turf."

Fortunately, the innovation team recognized that the T-shaped thinkers who generated the breakthrough innovation idea might also be helpful in building a prototype to test the solution with customers. But now they cast their net even further beyond their marketing agencies and dispenser manufacturers, and brought in software integrators, packaging designers, and supply chain consultants.

It was this wide assortment of divergent thinkers and doers that worked on defining the MVP. Their combined experience helped build a series of prototypes where each new prototype was quantifiably better than the previous one.

Their MVP criteria were clearly crafted. For the Decision Maker (i.e., the restaurant owner), the functionality required was concentrated syrup. This was necessary for the Decision Maker to adopt the innovation because it would allow him to expand his beverage menu and, consequently, make more money serving the most profitable item in his restaurant.

The User (i.e., the restaurant manager) also had a single functional requirement to automatically refill the restaurant's beverage inventory. This automation eliminated inventory tracking, ordering,

Coca-Cola Freestyle™
©*The Coca-Cola Company, all rights reserved*

reconciliation, and payment processing hassles. With these benefits delivered, the restaurant manager could redirect her attention to food preparation, overseeing staff performance, and ensuring guest satisfaction.

The Blocker (i.e., operations manager) wanted to make sure the system was self-monitoring. This functionality needed to be measured and had to produce a beverage that was within very narrow tolerance levels to ensure high quality beverages were being dispensed. This quality control capability would make or break the innovation.

The first several prototypes failed to work. However, this was not important. The goal was to learn what was possible. The syrup became more and more concentrated. This led to a smaller and smaller piece of equipment. It also led to more and more beverage options that could produce more and more sales.

The inventory tracking system was linked to the automatic ordering system. Over time, these systems were linked to the invoice system. Eventually, volume discounts and other adjustments were added as legacy IS systems were either modified or retired.

Unfortunately, the break-even analysis remains confidential. But if you live in the United States, you probably saw how the launch plan was executed. These innovative machines were first introduced at your local movie theater, then your neighborhood deli, then your favorite sandwich chain. Each location generated new insights on how to continuously improve the system.

Despite the complexity of the problem, the innovation team succeeded at creating the functionality that mattered most. Innovation seldom follows a straight path and this project was no exception. The Coca-Cola Freestyle dispensing system took a circuitous route to become a breakthrough innovation. But it has also proven to be one of the biggest innovations in The Coca-Cola Company's storied 100+ year history.

Map 1: Stress

List 10 stresses:

1. Running out of product
2. Takes too long to get product replaced
3. Lifting heavy 5-gallon containers
4. Storing bulky containers
5. Conducting daily maintenance
6. Inconsistent beverage quality
7. Limited drink offerings
8. Too long to get service
9. Reconciling invoices
10. Too much Coca-Cola Salespeople turnover

List 10 more stresses:

1. Can't track product delivery
2. High general delivery costs
3. Very high "emergency" delivery costs
4. High service costs
5. Reactive, not proactive, service
6. Slow service response time
7. Limited market share growth
8. Limited same store volume growth
9. High "churn" rate with Pepsico
10. High accounts receivable

When these stresses occur, what happens...

...behaviorally?

Continuous "fire drills"

Escalating costs

Hard to do business with

...emotionally?

Declining reliability and trust

Not customer focused

24/7 worrying

WHAT DOES THIS TELL YOU?

Current system is not financially sustainable

Map 2: Customer Experience

Journey Map of Restaurant Manager **trying to** serve high quality beverages.

Description of Step

Step 1	Step 2	Step 3	Step 4	Step 5
Order product	Receive, store, rotate product	Test beverage quality	Call for product delivery or service	Audit inventory, reconcile with invoices

On Stage

	Step 1	Step 2	Step 3	Step 4	Step 5
people	Customer Service Rep	Delivery Agent		Customer Service Rep	Sales Manager & Finance Manager
things	Order Management System	Delivery Ticket	Quality Assurance Guide	Repair Order	

Back Stage

	Step 1	Step 2	Step 3	Step 4	Step 5
people	Coca-Cola Bottler or Wholesale Distributor		Call Center Technicians	Coca-Cola Bottler or Wholesale Distributor	Audit Manager
things	Shipping Logistics System	Shipping Logistics System	Trouble-shooting knowledge base	Agent Dispatch System	Order Management & Accounts Receivable Systems

Map 3: Compensating Behaviors

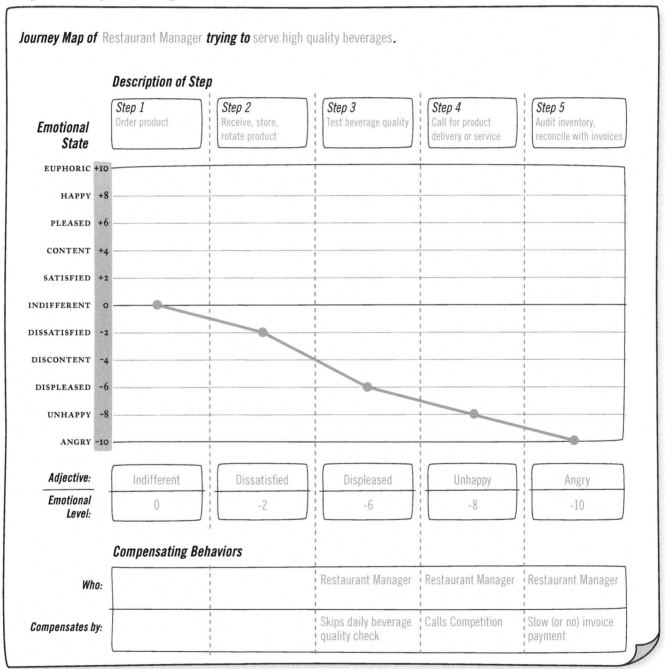

Journey Map of Restaurant Manager **trying to** serve high quality beverages.

Description of Step

	Step 1	Step 2	Step 3	Step 4	Step 5
Emotional State	Order product	Receive, store, rotate product	Test beverage quality	Call for product delivery or service	Audit inventory, reconcile with invoices

Emotional State scale:
- EUPHORIC +10
- HAPPY +8
- PLEASED +6
- CONTENT +4
- SATISFIED +2
- INDIFFERENT 0
- DISSATISFIED -2
- DISCONTENT -4
- DISPLEASED -6
- UNHAPPY -8
- ANGRY -10

Adjective:	Indifferent	Dissatisfied	Displeased	Unhappy	Angry
Emotional Level:	0	-2	-6	-8	-10

Compensating Behaviors

Who:			Restaurant Manager	Restaurant Manager	Restaurant Manager
Compensates by:			Skips daily beverage quality check	Calls Competition	Slow (or no) invoice payment

Map 4: Solutions

What ideas do you have already?

Increase size of product containers

What's the most efficient thing to do?

Shift delivery from bottlers and wholesale distributors to UPS

What's the easiest thing to do?

Proactively send out service agents to conduct quality assessments

What's the fastest thing to do?

Shrink the size of the product container from 5-gallons to 2.5 gallons

What's the industry-leading thing to do?

Create inventory and beverage quality self-monitoring dispenser

What's the provocative thing to do?

Offer 100+ beverages from one dispenser system

Map 5: Assumptions

Facts We Know	Facts We Don't Know but COULD know	Facts We Don't Know and CAN'T Know
Can't track product delivery	Can syrup be concentrated enough to create a package like an ink cartridge?	Cost of dispensing system
High general delivery costs		Costs of syrup cartridges
Very high "emergency" delivery costs	What's the minimum number of syrup cartridges needed to produce the maximum number of beverages?	Adoption rates of current customer base
High service costs	Can these syrup cartridges be shipped, tracked, and reported by UPS?	
Reactive, not proactive, service		
Slow service response time	Can a self-monitoring system be built to automatically reorder syrup cartridges?	
Limited market share growth	Can a self-monitoring system test quality on a scheduled basis?	
Limited same store volume growth	Can a self-monitoring system call for service when there's a problem?	
High "churn" rate with Pepsico		
High Accounts Receivable		

We could quickly gather data by:

Meet with Product Development

Meet with UPS

Check with equipment manufacturers

Check existing Customer Call Center infrastructure

Map 6: Allies

Potential Ally	1	2	3	4
Name:	Dispenser Company A	Dispenser Company B	Movie Theatre Customers	Small Sandwich Chains
Organization:				
Title:				
Role:				
Excited about innovation	7	5	9	7
Shares your vision	5	3	7	5
Sees immediate benefits	7	3	7	7
Has peer credibility	5	7	7	7
Willing to publically endorse you	9	9	8	8
total score:	31	25	38	34

Map 7: Value Proposition

Once upon a time...

Our prospective customer is a Restaurant Owner

who wants to serve high quality, high profit beverages, 24/7

SUDDENLY...

he finds that processes are complicated and time-consuming,

so he must constantly call to complain and get help.

And then...

He discovers an innovative, self-monitoring beverage dispenser connected to the Internet,

so he can now serve 100+ beverages, automatically order products, test beverage quality, and call for a service agent.

Map 8: Assets

What assets do you already have in your organization?

Product Development

Equipment Engineering

Equipment Service

Marketing

What assets have other industries used?

Business Process Mapping

User Experience Architects

Data Architects

What assets worked in previous innovations?

Broad Product Portfolio

Large Customer Base

What assets do you need to move quickly?

Dispenser Manufacturers

Innovation Consultants

What assets have you always wanted to work with?

Logistics Distributors

What new technology assets can you try?

Touch Screens

Internet Connectivity

Software Integrators

Packaging Designers

Map 9: Minimum Viable Product

The Decision Maker

This person... the Restaurant Owner

Needs this minimum functionality... concentrated syrup dispenser

So they can do these jobs... expand their beverage menu

That will result in these benefits... selling more high-profit beverages

The User

This person... the Restaurant Manager

Needs this minimum functionality... self-monitoring inventory and quality assurance

So they can do these jobs... serve high-quality beverages with no out-of-stock issues

That will result in these benefits... eliminate ordering, tracking, quality assurance monitoring, and reconciliation processes

The Blocker

This person... the Restaurant Operations Manager

Needs this minimum functionality... continuous dispenser connectivity

So they can do these jobs... measure and monitor performance 24/7

That will result in these benefits... lower operating costs and improved bottom line

Map 10: Cost Structure

CONFIDENTIAL

Startup Costs:	
Developer Fees	$_____
Consultant Fees	$_____
Agency Fees	$_____
Legal Fees	$_____
Other	$_____
	$_____
	$_____
	$_____
Total	$_____

RTB Fixed Costs:	Year 1	Year 2	Year 3
Marketing Salaries	$_____	$_____	$_____
Sales Salaries	$_____	$_____	$_____
Customer Support Salaries	$_____	$_____	$_____
Product Support Salaries	$_____	$_____	$_____
Marketing Programs	$_____	$_____	$_____
Training Programs	$_____	$_____	$_____
General & Admin.	$_____	$_____	$_____
Other	$_____	$_____	$_____
	$_____	$_____	$_____
Annual Total	$_____	$_____	$_____
Three-Year Total		$_____	

Break-even (Units) =

$$\frac{\text{Startup Costs} + \text{RTB Fixed Costs}}{(\text{Unit Price} - \text{Cost of Goods Sold Per Unit})}$$

Break-even (Revenue) =

$$\frac{\text{Startup Costs} + \text{RTB Fixed Costs}}{1 - (\text{Cost of Goods Sold Per Unit}/\text{Unit Price})}$$

RTB Variable Costs:	Year 1	Year 2	Year 3
Unit Average Cost	$_____	$_____	$_____

Map 11: Launch Plan

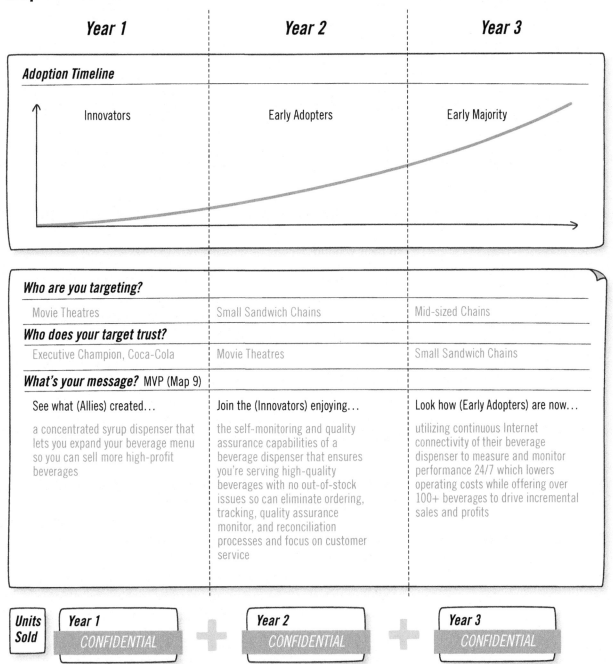

	Year 1	Year 2	Year 3

Adoption Timeline

Innovators | Early Adopters | Early Majority

Who are you targeting?

| Movie Theatres | Small Sandwich Chains | Mid-sized Chains |

Who does your target trust?

| Executive Champion, Coca-Cola | Movie Theatres | Small Sandwich Chains |

What's your message? MVP (Map 9)

See what (Allies) created...	Join the (Innovators) enjoying...	Look how (Early Adopters) are now...
a concentrated syrup dispenser that lets you expand your beverage menu so you can sell more high-profit beverages	the self-monitoring and quality assurance capabilities of a beverage dispenser that ensures you're serving high-quality beverages with no out-of-stock issues so can eliminate ordering, tracking, quality assurance monitor, and reconciliation processes and focus on customer service	utilizing continuous Internet connectivity of their beverage dispenser to measure and monitor performance 24/7 which lowers operating costs while offering over 100+ beverages to drive incremental sales and profits

Units Sold

Year 1		Year 2		Year 3
CONFIDENTIAL	+	CONFIDENTIAL	+	CONFIDENTIAL

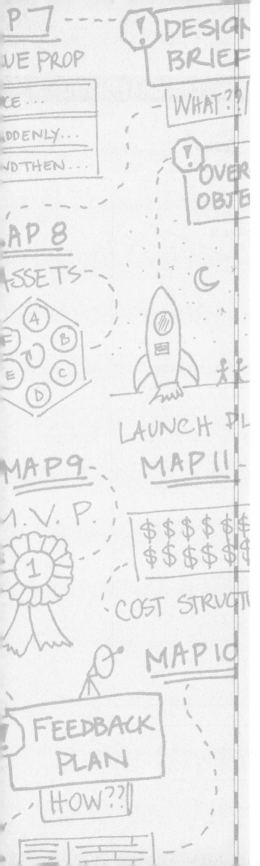

FRIENDS & FAMILY PLAN

Many manufacturers, retailers, hotels, and even airlines offer incentive discounts to selected groups of people affiliated with their organizations. Sometimes these incentive discounts are part of an employee's compensation package, or a human resources benefit, or some other plan to encourage employees to recommend an organization's products and/or services.

For example, automotive manufacturers frequently provide incentive discounts to "Friends and Family" of employees. Some automotive manufacturers even extend these incentive discounts to their vendors.

But these plans can be complex. Different groups of people may get different incentive discounts— some more, some less. And these incentive discounts may not be available on all makes and models (depending on vehicle inventory or production plans).

Let's say you were a family member of someone who worked at an auto manufacturer. You would be legible for the maximum incentive discount. If you were a friend of someone that worked at an auto manufacturer, then your incentive discount would be slightly lower. If you were a vendor, then your incentive discount would be even lower.

Regardless of your incentive discount level, your price would still be substantially below what you could get directly from a Dealer. More important, the price would be pre-negotiated so you could call up a Dealer, tell them you'd like a certain make, model, and trim, and they would sell you a vehicle off their lot or acquire it for you. The auto manufacturer guaranteed a profit to the Dealer and the sale would count toward the auto manufacturer's volume incentive program already in place with Dealers. It was a win/win/win.

Or at least, that was the idea. But there were several problems with the Friends and Family plan created by one Japanese auto manufacturer operating in North America. Employees had a hard time figuring out if their family or friends even qualified. If their family or friends did qualify, it could take up to five days before a special code would be issued to these prospective buyers.

When prospective buyers received their codes, they often asked the employees how much of a discount this code represented. Unfortunately, employees usually didn't know or struggled to explain the different incentive discount levels. Finally, employees never knew if their referral resulted in a sale so they never got the satisfaction of "closing a deal."

It was even harder for a prospective buyer. They didn't understand why they didn't get the maximum discount, or why the vehicle they wanted didn't qualify, or if other incentive discounts could be included, or what would be their final "out the door" price.

Dealers often tried to help, but they were not able to see the manufacturer's qualification criteria, or incentive discount levels, or qualifying vehicles. Operating in this information vacuum made it impossible to match the prospective buyer's vehicle request with the Dealer's inventory and price it appropriately.

The auto manufacturer tasked a marketing agency with issuing the special codes to prospective buyers and the agency was supposed to answer questions about the plan. Unfortunately, the agency (like the Dealers) often struggled to keep up with the ever-changing plan, and had the added burden of deducting local market limited-time-only incentive discounts from the final price.

Consequently, employees stopped making referrals. If a friend or family member did try to go through the process, they often gave up. In fact, less than 20% of friends and family members that received a special code actually purchased a vehicle, even though the plan offered the lowest possible price available in the market.

So the auto manufacturer hired a consulting firm, a software firm, and an automotive industry subject-matter expert to work with the auto manufacturer's marketing agency and internal cross-functional departments. This newly formed innovation team started their work by watching what prospective buyers were trying to do. They mapped each step of the process and asked the prospective buyers to assess the pain of each step.

Then the innovation team interviewed each prospective buyer a week after they started the shopping process. By this time, the prospective buyers had received their special code and should have contacted a Dealer. The team wanted to understand whether the buyers would be promoters of the plan so buyers were asked, "Would you recommend this plan to your friends and family? If yes, then why? If not, then why not?"

The vast majority responded that they would not recommend the plan because they couldn't get answers for three specific questions: 1). Do I qualify for a pre-negotiated price? 2). What is my pre-negotiated price? 3). Where can I buy the exact vehicle that I want?

Clearly, any innovative solution needed to address these fundamental questions. But more important, prospective buyers claimed they would have stopped shopping immediately if they just got what they needed with a few clicks of a mouse. The innovation team realized that when a buyer is ready to purchase, the auto manufacturer needed to act immediately and "close the deal."

This approach was very different from the "top of the sales funnel" vehicle awareness advertising role that corporate marketing traditionally performed at the auto manufacturer. Consequently, the innovation team decided it would be important to adopt a "bottom of the sales funnel" e-commerce mindset to define their key assumptions and identify the allies they needed.

With this mindset in place, the innovation team identified three important assumptions to be validated. Could they streamline the plan's eligibility questions? Could they use existing incentive discount data feeds to ensure accurate pricing? And could they match the buyer's desired vehicle with Dealer inventory in real-time?

Fortunately, there was an established internal department or advisory group to tackle each key assumption at the auto manufacturer. These allies would be critical to the innovation team's prototyping efforts since they controlled the data critical to transforming the plan.

Now the value proposition was clear:

"To friends and family looking to buy a new vehicle without the hassle of price shopping and searching inventory, the plan gives you the lowest pre-negotiated price available in the market for the car you desire so you save time and money while being treated like a V.I.P."

The next step of the innovation journey was to collect available assets. The innovation team found out who qualified for the plan and the specific criteria for each incentive discount. They collected information on every vehicle (i.e., pictures, video, color options, trim choices, specifications, etc.). They found a Vehicle Identification Number (VIN) software program that translated a VIN into the exact configuration of a vehicle, right down to the tire size. Most important, they obtained access to the inventory management system that showed which vehicles were on Dealer lots, which vehicles were being shipped to Dealers, and which vehicles were scheduled to be manufactured.

Armed with these assets, the innovation team reconvened to define the MVP. The software firm suggested using progressive profiling to qualify prospective buyers, i.e., new form fields are presented based on previously entered data. For example, if the prospective buyer claimed to be a family member of an auto manufacturer employee, then the prospective buyer would go down one qualification path with a unique set of questions to answer. But if the prospective buyer claimed to be an employee of the auto manufacturer vendor, then they would go down another qualification path and answer a different set of questions.

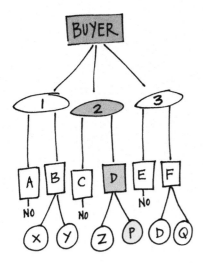

By using progressive profiling, the system could qualify a prospective buyer in real-time and present them with the appropriate discount. This process eliminated the need to present different discount levels. The prospective buyers would no longer think that they got a lower (or higher) discount than anyone else.

In order to prevent prospective buyers from fraudulently claiming they worked for a qualifying vendor, an email with an embedded link would be sent to a work email address to verify their employment. (Granted, this wasn't foolproof, but it was considered "good enough," since most participating companies were large organizations and most large organizations eliminate email access when an employee is no longer employed.)

With the eligibility issues addressed for The Blocker (i.e., the auto manufacturer), the innovation team moved on to selecting and configuring a vehicle while simultaneously aggregating all incentive discounts. Being able to determine the pre-negotiated price on eligible vehicles was critical for the Decision Maker (i.e., prospective buyer).

The auto manufacturer's marketing agency had already built vehicle configuration tools for a national website. These tools were reused on the Friends and Family website. By reusing existing assets, there were multiple benefits: consistency between the websites, common configuration experiences, and lower costs.

The innovation team tackled aggregating all of the possible incentive discounts next. The team learned that each local market was required to report the incentive discounts they offered, including the terms and conditions of the offer. The software firm created a database to combine this information with the national incentive discounts to show the prospective buyer the final and lowest price available, including when these incentive discounts would expire.

Lastly, the innovation team needed to tackle the needs of The User (i.e., the Dealers). This was a critical piece of the puzzle because unless there was transparency between the prospective buyers, the

auto manufacturer, and the Dealer, then there could easily be confusion when a prospective buyer called or showed up at the Dealership.

The innovation team worked with the Dealer Advisory Group (i.e., representatives of all Dealers) to establish a clear process for handling Friends and Family prospective buyers. Everyone agreed that the final vehicle configuration and pre-negotiated price needed to be shared simultaneously with all parties. The Dealers also realized that it was important for them to display their entire inventory in the Friends And Family system since less than 50% of prospective buyers actually purchase the vehicle they configure online.

The initial prototypes used static data rather than real-time data feeds. This sped up the feedback process. The vehicle configuration tools were only installed for a few models. This allowed senior management to understand how the process would work without spending time and money building out the functionality for the entire vehicle lineup.

The confirmation process—where prospective buyers received a summary of their order including vehicle configuration, final price, terms and conditions, Dealer phone number, and Google Map to the Dealer—was mapped out but not "live."

Using the auto manufacturer's existing stage-gate process of designing, creating, building and testing would have taken the innovation team 18-24 months. Instead, the prototype reviewed by the executive management team took 28 days to construct.

Once the project passed the "Go/No Go" decision point, the innovation team handed off the project to an IT commercialization team. The costs for the innovation team were $350,000, the costs for the commercialization team were $500,000, and the annual support costs of hosting, administering, and updating the website were $150,000.

The good news was that the new system no longer required six full-time employees at the marketing agency to manually produce and fulfill special codes or answer questions from prospective buyers and Dealers. This created an annual savings of $1,000,000 in agency fees so the innovation team reached break-even in the first year and actually produced a positive savings of over $800,000 each subsequent year.

The Friends And Family internal team launched the new website with an employee promotion that awarded employees for each vehicle sold. This allowed the team to trouble-shoot any questions or problems before the auto manufacturer's vendors were invited to use the new system. In the last phase of the launch plan, vendors were encouraged to share their positive experiences with their fellow work colleagues on social media.

The auto manufacturer projected Friends And Family sales to generate $60,000,000 in incremental annual gross profit over three years. Not bad for 90 days of innovation!

Map 1: Stress

List 10 prospective customer stresses:

1. Do I qualify for a discount?
2. How much is my discount?
3. Why don't I get the maximum discount?
4. What vehicles are eligible?
5. Why isn't the vehicle I want eligible?
6. What is my discounted price vs. MSRP?
7. Does my price include local incentives?
8. What is my final "out-the-door" price?
9. Where can I buy my vehicle?
10. How can I get what I'm promised?

List 10 Dealer stresses:

1. Don't know qualification criteria
2. Don't know different discount levels
3. Don't know what discount was offered
4. Don't know which vehicles are eligible
5. Don't know why some vehicles are ineligible
6. Don't know discounted price vs. MSRP
7. Don't know what local incentives to include
8. Can't provide "out-the-door" prices
9. Can't display current inventory
10. Can't offer different model or trim options

When these stresses occur, what happens...

...behaviorally?

Loss of highly interested buyers

Escalating agency costs

Slows Dealer transition to digital marketing

...emotionally?

High frustration with Dealers

Reinforce negative stereotypes

Undermine "hassle-free" promise

WHAT DOES THIS TELL YOU?

We're losing predisposed buyers likely to be long-term loyal supporters

Map 2: Customer Experience

Journey Map of Friends and Family Memebers *trying to* buy a new vehicle.

Description of Step

Step 1	Step 2	Step 3	Step 4	Step 5	Step 6
Learn about program	Qualify for program	Wait 5 days for special code	Configure a vehicle on national website	Call Dealers to find desired vehicle	Try to get "out-of-door" price

On Stage

	people	Auto Manufacturer				Dealer	Dealer
	things	Friends & Family Website	Website Submission Form	Email Verification	National Website		

Back Stage

	people		Agency Processes Submission Form	Agency Activates Special Code			
	things		Random Code Generator	Discount Database			

Map 3: Compensating Behaviors

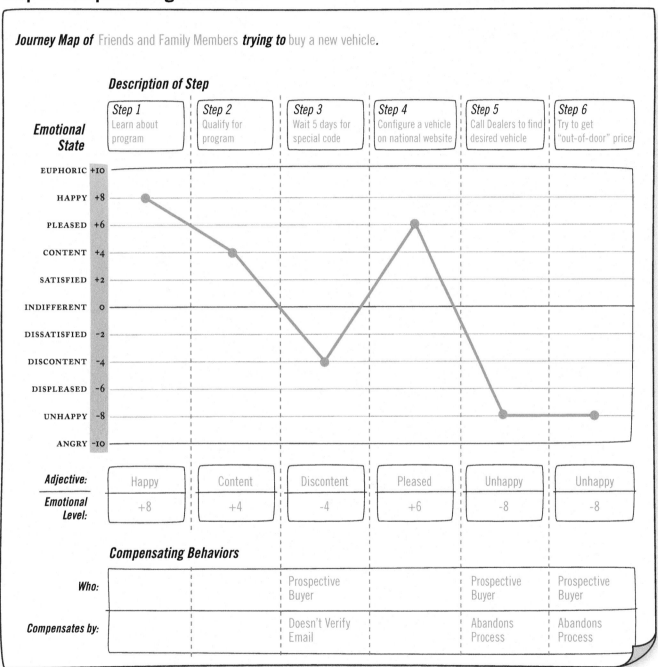

Journey Map of Friends and Family Members **trying to** buy a new vehicle.

Description of Step

Emotional State

Step 1	Step 2	Step 3	Step 4	Step 5	Step 6
Learn about program	Qualify for program	Wait 5 days for special code	Configure a vehicle on national website	Call Dealers to find desired vehicle	Try to get "out-of-door" price

Emotional State						
EUPHORIC +10						
HAPPY +8						
PLEASED +6						
CONTENT +4						
SATISFIED +2						
INDIFFERENT 0						
DISSATISFIED -2						
DISCONTENT -4						
DISPLEASED -6						
UNHAPPY -8						
ANGRY -10						

	Step 1	Step 2	Step 3	Step 4	Step 5	Step 6
Adjective:	Happy	Content	Discontent	Pleased	Unhappy	Unhappy
Emotional Level:	+8	+4	-4	+6	-8	-8

Compensating Behaviors

	Step 1	Step 2	Step 3	Step 4	Step 5	Step 6
Who:			Prospective Buyer		Prospective Buyer	Prospective Buyer
Compensates by:			Doesn't Verify Email		Abandons Process	Abandons Process

Map 4: Solutions

What ideas do you have already?

Update Friends & Family website with Dealer website links

What's the most efficient thing to do?

Real-time eligibility qualification

What's the easiest thing to do?

Put a link on national website to Friends & Family website

What's the fastest thing to do?

Rebuild website on Salesforce.com platform to connect to existing customer call centers

What's the industry-leading thing to do?

Match desired configured vehicle to real-time dealer inventory

What's the provocative thing to do?

Aggregate all incentive discounts to calculate final "out-the-door" price

Map 5: Assumptions

Facts We Know	Facts We Don't Know but COULD know	Facts We Don't Know and CAN'T Know
We can use existing vehicle assets (e.g., images, video, specifications, etc.) We can use existing vehicle configuration tools We can use existing software platform to simultaneously present information to prospective buyers, Dealers, and HQ	How can progressive profiling match up with all qualification criteria? How can all incentive discounts be aggregated? How can we match up a prospective buyer's configured vehicle to Dealer inventory?	Increase in Friends and Family sales conversion rate Willingness of Friends and Family to build awareness of program using social media

We could quickly gather data by:

Mapping out eligibility criteria and corresponding incentives

Find out how national and local incentives are tracked and monitored

Discover how inventory is tracked from factory to distributor to Dealer to customer

Map 6: Allies

Potential Ally	1	2	3	4
Name:	Dealer Advisory Board	Marketing Agency	Finance & Incentive Dept.	Inventory Management
Organization:				
Title:				
Role:				
Excited about innovation	7	7	8	5
Shares your vision	8	3	7	6
Sees immediate benefits	7	3	7	5
Has peer credibility	9	7	7	9
Willing to publically endorse you	5	3	6	6
total score:	36	23	35	31

Map 7: Value Proposition

Once upon a time...

Our customer is a Friends and Family Member

who wants to save time and money with a hassle-free buying experience.

SUDDENLY...

he finds that getting qualified is a confusing multi-step process,

so he must call Dealers to find a vehicle and get an "out-the-door" price.

And then...

He discovers progressive profiling, online vehicle configuration, aggregated incentive discounts, "out-the-door" pricing, inventory availability, vehicle and price confirmation.

so he's able to set a test drive appointment, pre-qualify for financing, evaluate trade-in value like a true V.I.P.

Map 8: Assets

What assets do you already have in your organization?

Vehicle Information

Vehicle MSRP

National Incentive Discounts

Finance Terms & Conditions

What assets have other industries used?

Vehicle Identification Number (VIN) Software

What assets worked in previous innovations?

Vehicle configuration tools

What assets do you need to move quickly?

Flexible, scalable software platform

What assets have you always wanted to work with?

Progressive profiling integrated into master customer database

What new technology assets can you try?

Real-time image and information updates

Map 9: Minimum Viable Product

The Decision Maker

This person... the Friends & Family Member

Needs this minimum functionality... real-time incentive discount off MSRP on eligible vehicles.

So they can do these jobs... buy a vehicle

That will result in these benefits... hassle-free negotiation

---

The User

This person... the Dealer

Needs this minimum functionality... final "out-the-door" pricing on inventory

So they can do these jobs... match buyer with inventory on the lot or in-transit

That will result in these benefits... predisposed buyer to visit Dealership

---

The Blocker

This person... the Auto Manufacturer

Needs this minimum functionality... error-free eligibility process

So they can do these jobs... offer V.I.P. status

That will result in these benefits... drive millions of potential buyers to Dealerships

Map 10: Cost Structure

Startup Costs:	Year 1
Engineering Fees	$_____
Developer Fees	$ 175k
Consultant Fees	$ 175k
Agency Fees	$_____
Legal Fees	$_____
Other	$_____
	$_____
	$_____
	$_____
Total	$ 350k

RTB Fixed Costs:	Year 1	Year 2	Year 3
Marketing Salaries	$_____	$_____	$_____
Sales Salaries	$_____	$_____	$_____
Customer Support Salaries	$_____	$_____	$_____
Product Support Salaries	$_____	$_____	$_____
Marketing Programs	$_____	$_____	$_____
Training Programs	$_____	$_____	$_____
General & Admin.	$_____	$_____	$_____
Other	$_____	$_____	$_____
	$_____	$_____	$_____
Annual Total	$ 650k	$ 150k	$ 200k
Three-Year Total			$ 1.0 million

Break-even (Units) =

$$\frac{\text{Startup Costs} + \text{RTB Fixed Costs}}{(\text{Unit Price} - \text{Cost of Goods Sold Per Unit})}$$

Break-even (Revenue) =

$$\frac{\text{Startup Costs} + \text{RTB Fixed Costs}}{1 - (\text{Cost of Goods Sold Per Unit} / \text{Unit Price})}$$

RTB Variable Costs:	Year 1	Year 2	Year 3
Annualized Savings	$1.0 million	$1.0 million	$1.0 million

Map 11: Launch Plan

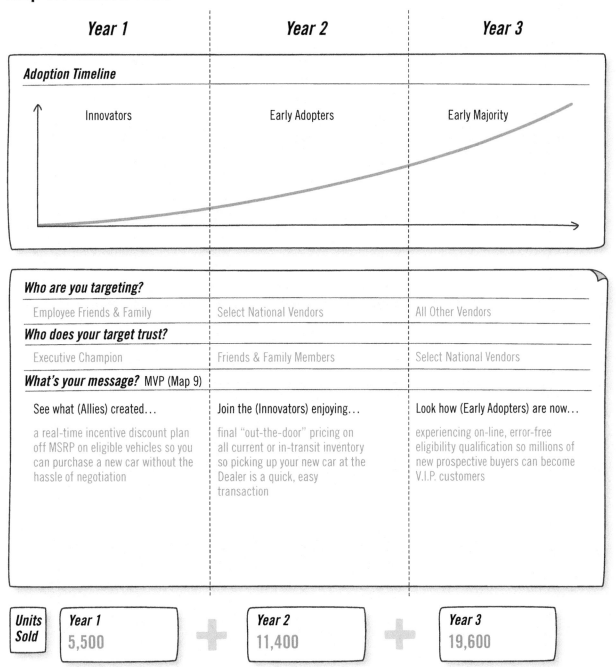

	Year 1	Year 2	Year 3
Adoption Timeline	Innovators	Early Adopters	Early Majority

Who are you targeting?		
Employee Friends & Family	Select National Vendors	All Other Vendors

Who does your target trust?		
Executive Champion	Friends & Family Members	Select National Vendors

What's your message? MVP (Map 9)

See what (Allies) created…	Join the (Innovators) enjoying…	Look how (Early Adopters) are now…
a real-time incentive discount plan off MSRP on eligible vehicles so you can purchase a new car without the hassle of negotiation	final "out-the-door" pricing on all current or in-transit inventory so picking up your new car at the Dealer is a quick, easy transaction	experiencing on-line, error-free eligibility qualification so millions of new prospective buyers can become V.I.P. customers

Units Sold	Year 1	Year 2	Year 3
	5,500	11,400	19,600

MOBILE DIGITAL MEDIA

Entrepreneurs have their own set of innovation challenges. Fortunately, the IN-90 Framework can be used with small startups as well as established large corporations.

One advantage of being an entrepreneur is the ability to move quickly. One disadvantage is limited capital. This makes innovation easier and riskier at the same time. Mobile Digital Media (MDM) is an excellent example of how a small startup had to move quickly and make a big financial bet. If they lost the bet, they'd be out of business.

MDM was a publisher of software applications for mobile devices and was the precursor to the Apple App Store. But when MDM started, "smartphones" weren't available yet. MDM was producing software for Personal Digital Assistants (PDAs) that had a global installed base of 20 million devices equally split between the Microsoft and Palm operating systems.

Back then, mobile devices had very little RAM, hard drive storage, or processing power. Software applications had to be placed on Secure Digital (SD) or MultiMedia Cards (MMC) that were inserted into the device. These cards were sold at retail as accessories to the mobile devices. But retailers were tough customers; they demanded a wide selection of applications to run on any operating system and they expected high sales turnover of every application.

MDM understood these retailer demands and quickly acquired content from Electronic Arts, Sega, Rand McNally, Webster's Dictionary and Thesaurus, and Microsoft Xbox to create applications that ran on multiple operating systems. These applications were then adapted and tested to be compatible with hardware from HP, Toshiba, Dell, Nokia, Motorola, Palm, and more.

Retailers loved the new, consolidated product lineup and orders piled in. Soon MDM saw its products in Best Buy, Office Depot, Staples, Amazon.com, Dell.com, and many other consumer electronic retailers.

But just as quickly as success struck, problems popped up. Consumers complained that MDM software applications wouldn't always run when devices received an operating system update. These updates happened frequently, so it wasn't unusual for the operating systems to "break" the applications.

Consumers were also frustrated that the applications were so expensive, i.e., $15-20, and were on cards that were so small. Ironically, this turned out to be a problem because the more popular the applications on the card, the more the cards were inserted into the device. The more times the card was popped in and out of the device, the more likely it was to lose or misplace the small card.

Finally, new hardware devices were being rapidly introduced, including the first smartphones, so consumers were reluctant to buy applications for a mobile device that might become obsolete in the near future.

MDM was at a crossroads. With limited capital, their management had to decide what to do. Should they try to tie up content and sell the company for its intellectual property? Should they downsize the company and milk the profits out of the existing business? Should they create a platform for developers to submit, distribute, and sell their applications? Was there another option?

The CEO was a "deal maker" and thought he could find a hardware manufacturer to buy the company. The COO was a "controller" and didn't want to consider any option that affected the supply chain he had built over the last 12-18 months. The rest of the leadership team thought they should talk to consumers and see if they could glean any insights to guide their next steps.

Unable to reach a consensus, the group split up and went their different ways. The CEO went on the road to find a "White Knight." The COO continued to pick, pack, and ship cards while handling an increasing amount of retailer returns. The remainder of the team started interviewing consumers.

The consumer perspective was eye-opening. These people identified themselves as "geeks and freaks." They took great pride in being innovative. While they enjoyed MDM applications like Wine Spectator and Webster's Crossword Puzzle, these applications didn't allow them to show the merits of being innovative.

They wanted a set of applications that made them productive regardless of where they were. They didn't want to have to rely on Wi-Fi or other means of connectivity. In their words, they wanted to be "Always On."

When probed, these consumers explained that they used their mobile devices primarily for work. They traveled frequently and often felt out of touch with their offices. They needed to be able to view, create, and edit documents, especially Microsoft Office applications like Word, Excel, and PowerPoint.

But these applications had to be lightweight because the devices were still short on memory. To prevent confusion when switching from Word to Excel to PowerPoint, core functions like "cut and paste" and "save" had to use the same buttons on the mobile device. (Touch screens weren't widely available yet.) Finally, the applications had to be updateable since the operating systems and hardware devices were still in continuous flux.

The key assumptions flowed from this solution. Specifically, could the Microsoft Office applications be streamlined to address the mobile device limitations? Could the applications be mapped to a common set of hardware buttons to make devices interchangeable? Could software updates occur by downloading just the new code and not all of the Microsoft Office code?

MDM clearly needed to create allies within the Microsoft Mobile Group, Partner Group, and Product Development Group. MDM also needed an ally to conduct quality assurance since it was struggling to access the latest operating systems and devices. Lastly, MDM needed to establish relationships with mobile application download sites that were quickly replacing retailers as software application distributors.

Now the MDM Value Proposition needed to be completely rewritten. It was no longer a publisher of mobile applications for anyone owning a mobile device. It was now targeting mobile information workers stressed out by being disconnected from the office. For these people, MDM would provide the capabilities to view, create, and edit Microsoft Office documents on their phones so they could be more productive and responsive.

Even though MDM was a small startup, it still had several assets. It had an existing relationship with Microsoft because it had already published the Xbox game, "Age of Empires." It also had a visionary CTO with deep technical expertise. Finally, it had a Quality Assurance group with a meticulous methodology for testing.

MDM knew it was now time to define the MVP. This was particularly important since it meant working with the 800-pound gorilla known as Microsoft. MDM positioned its MVP as simply a software development "experiment" rather than a retail product. This allowed MDM to leverage its existing relationship with the Microsoft Mobile Group without needing to establish another, more formal, one.

MDM started by trying to strip down the Microsoft Word application to work on the limited capabilities of mobile devices. Many prototypes were rapidly developed. It quickly became obvious that the desktop version and the mobile version needed to be separate but compatible applications. There were too many desktop QWERTY keyboard and command functions for the existing application to work on many mobile devices.

This prototype experimentation prompted the Microsoft Mobile Group to reach out to several mobile phone manufactures to learn about their hardware product roadmaps. All parties agreed that there was benefit in sharing their respective plans for the future.

With non-disclosure agreements firmly in place, the roadmaps were exchanged. The manufacturer roadmaps revealed significant increases in RAM, hard drive capacity, and processing power coming in the next 12-24 months.

This changed the direction of MDM. They decided to develop and launch the Microsoft Office applications directly on hardware device platforms. This would allow MDM to focus its scarce resources and leverage the existing relationships Microsoft Mobile had with device manufacturers. Microsoft Mobile was eager to help expand its footprint in the emerging mobile phone marketplace, where 100 million devices would be built the following year.

The economics of this change in direction were significant. The wholesale cost of an SD or MMC to retailers was $12.95 and the Cost of Goods Sold (including a promotion and buyback allowance for retailers) was $8.95, so each SD or MMC unit sold generated a Gross Profit of $4 or 31%. But when Microsoft Office applications were installed directly on a smartphone, the wholesale price of these products was $1, but the Cost of Goods Sold was only $.15 so each sale generated a Gross Profit of $.85 or 85%.

Obviously, this new direction would greatly improve their gross profit margin for MDM, but its revenue per unit sold would be much lower. This is where MDM had to make its big bet; should it

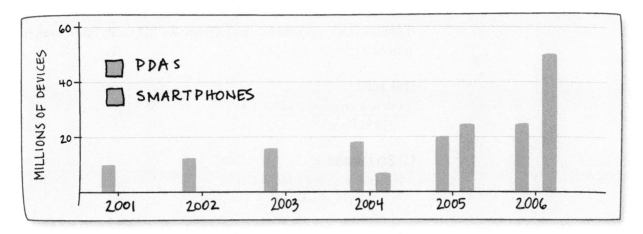

continue to pursue the proven, established PDA market, or pursue
the emerging, unknown smartphone market?

The PDA installed total global market was 25 million devices.
Smartphone manufacturing plans for the next year called for the
production of 100 million devices. There were also projections
of a smartphone installed base of almost 1 billion devices in 7 years.
(This 2007 projection proved to be incredibly accurate with an
installed base of over 1 billion smartphones in 2014.)

MDM decided to build financial models for the two strategic
directions under consideration. One model would assume MDM
stayed in the PDA software application business, and the other
assumed it would move quickly to the smartphone installed platform
application business.

Unlike a large organization, small startups usually include all
of their expenses when calculating their innovation costs. This was
particularly relevant for MDM management as they were
pivoting their entire business model to a new one. By including all
expenses in the analysis, the shareholders gained clarity on both
their sales goals and risk profile.

MDM had 30 full-time employees and the average annual
compensation was roughly $100,000 per employee.
Overhead expenses including benefits were approximately 20% of
salary expenses.

If MDM stuck with publishing software for PDAs, its break-even in units and revenue would be:

900k units =
$$\frac{\$3.0 \text{ million salary} + \$600k \text{ OH}}{(\$12.95 \text{ Price} - \$8.95 \text{ COGS})}$$

$11.6m revenue =
$$\frac{\$3.0 \text{ million salary} + \$600k \text{ OH}}{1 - (\$8.95 \div \$12.95)}$$

If MDM switched to publishing software for smartphones, its break-even in units and revenue would be:

4.2 million units =
$$\frac{\$3.0 \text{ million salary} + \$600k \text{ OH}}{(\$1.00 \text{ Price} - \$0.15 \text{ COGS})}$$

$4.2m revenue =
$$\frac{\$3.0 \text{ million salary} + \$600k \text{ OH}}{1 - (\$0.15 \div \$1.00)}$$

There were many sleepless nights as MDM struggled to decide its future. Fortunately, Microsoft proved to be a strong partner and encouraged several smartphone manufacturers to load the Microsoft Office applications on future phone platforms. With these tentative assurances, MDM changed its business model and product offerings.

In the end, the launch plan was straightforward. MDM installed the Microsoft Office applications on Nokia smartphones in Europe, Motorola smartphones in the U.S., and Palm smartphones around the world.

MDM survived because it recognized that speed matters.

Map 1: Stress

List 10 prospective customer stresses:

1. Don't know how the app works
2. Don't know if the app is compatible
3. Don't know how to get app updates
4. Afraid to lose SD/MMC card
5. High cost of card
6. Hard to find cards at retail
7. Want cards to work in multiple devices
8. Want trial versions
9. Want productivity applications
10. Want familiar, predictable experiences

List 10 retailer stresses:

1. Want operating system-agnostic apps
2. Want high sales turnover apps
3. Want wide variety of apps
4. Want promotional funding
5. Want right to return unsold apps
6. Want consignment terms
7. Want theft protection packaging
8. Want buyer protection packaging
9. Want 24/7 customer service
10. Want download site for updates & fixes

When these stresses occur, what happens...

...behaviorally?

Too much inventory

Too many devices to test

Too many operating systems to test

...emotionally?

Too unreliable with hardware proliferation

Titles too risky to stock

WHAT DOES THIS TELL YOU?

Our business model must change

Map 2: Customer Experience

Journey Map of PDA Owners **trying to** buy software applications.

Description of Step

Step 1	Step 2	Step 3	Step 4	Step 5
Learn about app	Find app at retail	Check compatibility with device and OS	Purchase app	Download app updates and fixes

On Stage

	people				
	Bloggers and Reviewers	Retailer		Retailer	

	things				
	Blogs and print/online articles	Point of Sale display	Packaging	Return Policies	

Back Stage

	people				
		In-store merchandiser			

	things				
	Ratings and Reviews	Point of Sale shipping		Product Inventory System	OS update quality assurance

Map 3: Compensating Behaviors

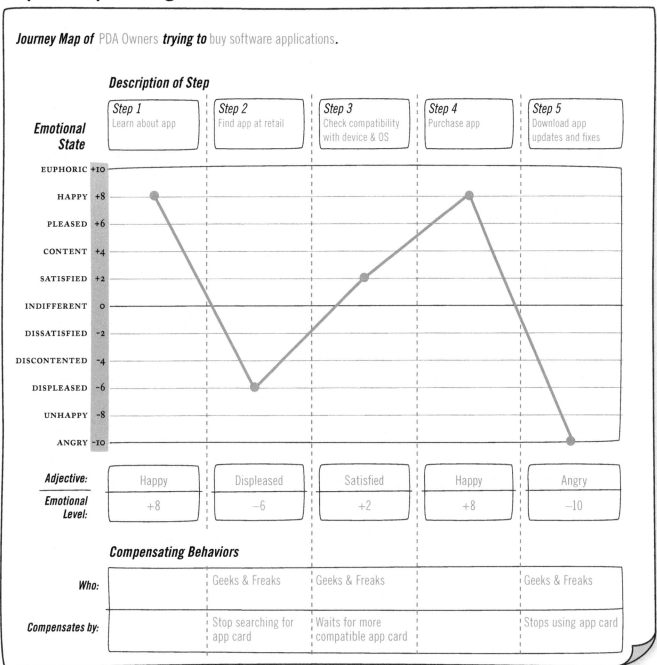

Journey Map of PDA Owners ***trying to*** buy software applications.

Description of Step

	Step 1	Step 2	Step 3	Step 4	Step 5
Emotional State	Learn about app	Find app at retail	Check compatibility with device & OS	Purchase app	Download app updates and fixes

Emotional State scale:

EUPHORIC	+10
HAPPY	+8
PLEASED	+6
CONTENT	+4
SATISFIED	+2
INDIFFERENT	0
DISSATISFIED	-2
DISCONTENTED	-4
DISPLEASED	-6
UNHAPPY	-8
ANGRY	-10

	Step 1	Step 2	Step 3	Step 4	Step 5
Adjective:	Happy	Displeased	Satisfied	Happy	Angry
Emotional Level:	+8	-6	+2	+8	-10

Compensating Behaviors

	Step 1	Step 2	Step 3	Step 4	Step 5
Who:		Geeks & Freaks	Geeks & Freaks		Geeks & Freaks
Compensates by:		Stop searching for app card	Waits for more compatible app card		Stops using app card

Map 4: Solutions

What ideas do you have already?

Strip down applications to be downloadble

What's the most efficient thing to do?

Publish Microsoft Office mobile apps

What's the easiest thing to do?

Focus on e-commerce distribution channels

What's the fastest thing to do?

Lay off 80% of employees until hardware catches up to software

What's the industry-leading thing to do?

Build an app store platform open to developers

What's the provocative thing to do?

License game, reference, mapping, productivity content and sell company to hardware manufacturer

Map 5: Assumptions

Facts We Know	Facts We Don't Know but COULD know	Facts We Don't Know and CAN'T Know
Proliferation of new hardware devices	How large are the current Microsoft Office applications?	Adoption rate of Smartphone hardware
Continuous updates to Operating System software	Can desktop versions of Microsoft Office be converted to mobile applications?	Most desired Smartphone applications
No industry standards for developing software applications	What are smartphone manufacturers' product road maps?	Pricing model for applications in 3 – 5 years
	What are smartphone manufacturers' installation requirements?	
	How can updates and fixes be delivered? Over the air? Synched? Both?	

We could quickly gather data by:

Working with Microsoft to gain access to their Software Development Kit (SDK)

Map 6: Allies

Potential Ally	1	2	3	4	5
Organization:	Microsoft Mobile Group	Microsoft Partner Group	Microsoft Product Development Group	Quality Assurance Firm	Mobile App Download Websites
Title:					
Role:					
Excited about innovation	8	7	6	8	7
Shares your vision	7	7	5	7	7
Sees immediate benefits	7	8	7	7	7
Has peer credibility	9	8	7	7	7
Willing to publically endorse you	5	5	5	6	3
total score:	36	35	30	36	31

Map 7: Value Proposition

> ### *Once upon a time...*
> Our customer is a Mobile Information Worker
>
> who wants to respond to questions and/or requests in real time.

> ### *SUDDENLY...*
> he finds that he can only read emails and PDF attachments,
>
> so he must respond with extensive emails or lengthy voicemails.

> ### *And then...*
> He discovers he can type new copy, cut and paste, and track changes with Microsoft Word, Excel, PowerPoint and Outlook
>
> so he's able to view documents, edit documents and create new documents.

Map 8: Assets

What assets do you already have in your organization?

Microsoft Mobile and Partner Group relationships

What assets have other industries used?

Online Bloggers

Print Reviewers

What assets worked in previous innovations?

CTO

Product Development

QA Team

What assets do you need to move quickly?

Dedicated Microsoft Account Manager

What assets have you always wanted to work with?

Software Code Decompilers

What new technology assets can you try?

Mobile Software Publishing Platforms

Map 9: Minimum Viable Product

The Decision Maker

This person... the Mobile Information Worker

Needs this minimum functionality... to view, edit, and create documents

So they can do these jobs... to provide input and feedback on time-sensitive documents

That will result in these benefits... higher productivity and lower stress

The User

This person... smartphone manufacturers

Needs this minimum functionality... lightweight Microsoft Office applications

So they can do these jobs... install applications directly on the device

That will result in these benefits... built-in, highly desired productivity applications

The Blocker

This person... Microsoft Product Group

Needs this minimum functionality... to maintain Microsoft Office Application integrity

So they can do these jobs... transfer desktop user knowledge to mobile devices

That will result in these benefits... rapid acceptance of mobile devices as indispensable productivity tools

Map 10: Cost Structure

RTB Fixed Costs:	Year 1	Year 2	Year 3
Marketing Salaries	$_____	$_____	$_____
Sales Salaries	$_____	$_____	$_____
Customer Support Salaries	$_____	$_____	$_____
Product Support Salaries	$_____	$_____	$_____
Marketing Programs	$_____	$_____	$_____
Training Programs	$_____	$_____	$_____
General & Admin.	$_____	$_____	$_____
Other	$_____	$_____	$_____
	$_____	$_____	$_____
Annual Total	$ 3.6 million	$ 3.6 million	$ 3.6 million
Three-Year Total			$ 10.8 million

RTB Variable Costs:	Year 1	Year 2	Year 3
SD/MMC Unit Avg. Cost	$ 8.95	$ 8.95	$ 8.95

SD/MMC Units

Break-even (Units) = 900k

$$\frac{\$3.0 \text{ million salary} + \$600k \text{ OH}}{(\$12.95 \text{ Price} - \$8.95 \text{ COGS})}$$

Break-even (Revenue) = $11.6m

$$\frac{\$3.0 \text{ million salary} + \$600k \text{ OH}}{1 - (\$8.95 \text{ COGS}/\$12.95 \text{ Unit Price})}$$

Install Units

Break-even (Units) = 4.2 million

$$\frac{\$3.0 \text{ million salary} + \$600k \text{ OH}}{(\$1.00 \text{ Price} - \$0.15 \text{ COGS})}$$

Break-even (Revenue) = $4.2m

$$\frac{\$3.0 \text{ million salary} + \$600k \text{ OH}}{1 - (\$0.15 \text{ COGS}/\$1.00 \text{ Unit Price})}$$

Map 11: Launch Plan

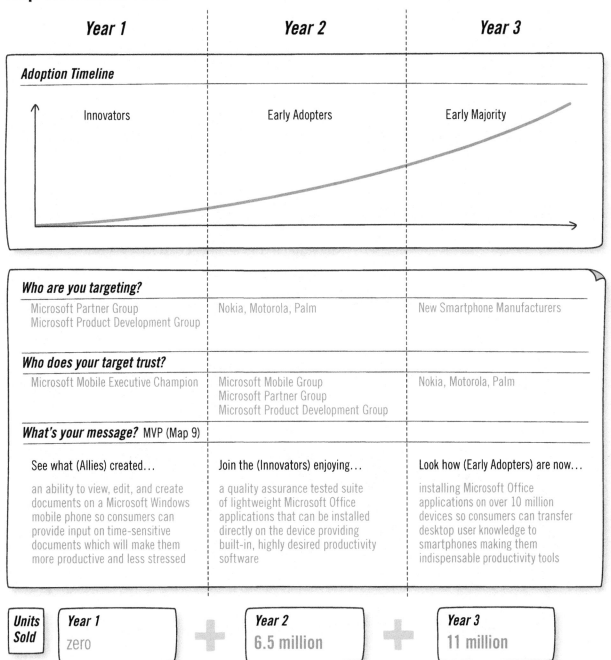

	Year 1	Year 2	Year 3

Adoption Timeline

Innovators — Early Adopters — Early Majority

Who are you targeting?

Year 1	Year 2	Year 3
Microsoft Partner Group Microsoft Product Development Group	Nokia, Motorola, Palm	New Smartphone Manufacturers

Who does your target trust?

Year 1	Year 2	Year 3
Microsoft Mobile Executive Champion	Microsoft Mobile Group Microsoft Partner Group Microsoft Product Development Group	Nokia, Motorola, Palm

What's your message? MVP (Map 9)

Year 1	Year 2	Year 3
See what (Allies) created...	Join the (Innovators) enjoying...	Look how (Early Adopters) are now...
an ability to view, edit, and create documents on a Microsoft Windows mobile phone so consumers can provide input on time-sensitive documents which will make them more productive and less stressed	a quality assurance tested suite of lightweight Microsoft Office applications that can be installed directly on the device providing built-in, highly desired productivity software	installing Microsoft Office applications on over 10 million devices so consumers can transfer desktop user knowledge to smartphones making them indispensable productivity tools

Units Sold

Year 1		Year 2		Year 3
zero	+	6.5 million	+	11 million

FINAL THOUGHTS
GOING BEYOND

INSPIRATIONAL READING

INTERNET INSIGHTS

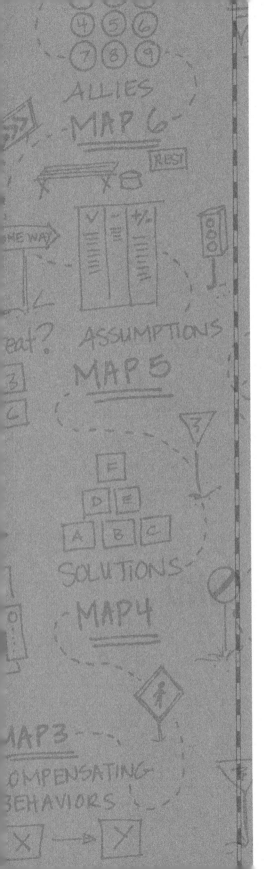

INSPIRATIONAL READING

There are worse crimes than burning books. One of them is not reading them. — Ray Bradbury, Author

I love to read because each new book provides a fresh perspective on both complex and simple ideas. I believe continuously reading keeps the creative sparks firing and enriches your world immeasurably. Here are some of my favorites that have inspired me and stretched my imagination.

Read these great books. Learn what others are doing. Find out what's next. Discover best practices. You never know what may lead to your breakthrough innovation.

The Innovation Killer: How What We Know Limits What We Can Imagine—And What Smart Companies Are Doing About It
by Cynthia Barton Rabe

Illustrates why companies that rely on "what we know" and "the way we do things here" to speed decision-making and maintain order will never be able to innovate.

Creative People Must Be Stopped:
6 Ways We Kill Innovation (Without Even Trying)
by David A. Owens

Identifies six types of constraints (individual, group, organizational, industry, societal, technological) that keep new creative ideas from being developed.

Creative Confidence: Unleashing
The Creative Potential Within Us All
by Tom Kelley and David Kelley

Provides specific strategies and practices to unleash the creative spark within us all.

*The Lean Startup: How Today's Entrepreneurs
Use Continuous Innovation to Create Radically
Successful Businesses*
by Eric Ries

New York Times Bestseller on rapid prototyping to
shorten product development cycles and how iterative
innovation helps discover what customers really want.

*The Design of Business: Why Design Thinking
Is The Next Competitive Advantage*
by Roger Martin

Explains how Design Thinking transforms an
unexplainable problem to a replicable success formula.

*Creative Intelligence: Harnessing the Power
to Create, Connect, and Inspire*
by Bruce Nussbaum

Explores Creative Intelligence as a new form of
cultural literacy and a method for driving innovation
and sparking startup capitalism.

*Steal An Artist: 10 Things Nobody
Told You About Being Creative*
by Austin Kleon

Suggests that nothing is original, so it's imperative
to learn through others, remix, and reimagine
creating your own path.

*The Accidental Creative: How To Be
Brilliant At A Moment's Notice*
by Todd Henry

Learn how to incorporate practices that instill a sense
of structure, rhythm, and purpose into your hectic
business life.

*101 Design Methods: A Structured Approach
for Driving Innovation in Your Organization*
by Vijay Kumar

Outlines how to approach the practice of creating new
products, services, and customer experiences as a
science.

*344 Questions: The Creative Person's Do-It-Yourself
Guide to Insight, Survival, and Artistic Fulfillment*
by Stephan G. Bucher

A collection of thought provoking questions to dig
deeply into human problems.

*Why Not? How To Use Everyday Ingenuity
To Solve Problems Big and Small*
by Barry Nalebuff and Ian Ayres

A primer on how true discovery consists of seeing what
everyone else has seen but thinking what nobody else
has thought.

Damn Good Advice (for people with talent!)
by George Lois

No-holds-barred, in-your-face advice and life lessons
from one of the original Mad Men and acclaimed
cultural provocateur.

**Made To Stick: Why Some Ideas
Survive and Others Die**
by Chip Heath and Dan Heath

Learn about the anatomy of ideas that stick, such
as the "human scale principle," the "Velcro Theory
of Memory," and "curiosity gaps."

**Making Ideas Happen: Overcoming
the Obstacles Between Vision and Reality**
by Scott Belsky

A helpful and practical analysis of why some creative
teams are highly productive while others fail.

**Strategy From The Outside In:
Profiting From Customer Value**
by George Day and Christine Moorman

How companies with an outside-in view focused on
customer value grow revenue, profit, and shareholder
value in good times and bad.

**Good Strategy and Bad Strategy:
The Difference and Why It Matters**
by Richard Rumelt

Explains why a good strategy is a specific and coherent
response utilizing nine sources of power to overcome
obstacles to progress.

Business Model Generation
by Alexander Osterwalder and Yves Pigneur

A handbook for visionaries, game changers, and
challengers striving to defy outmoded business models
and design tomorrow's winners.

**Predictably Irrational: The Hidden Forces
That Shape Our Decisions**
by Dan Ariely

Learn why we consistently overpay, underestimate,
procrastinate—and why these misguided behaviors are
systematic and predictable.

Switch: How To Change Things When Change Is Hard
by Chip Heath and Dan Heath

See how the tension between the rational mind and
emotional mind can be harnessed to create change
quickly like flipping a "switch."

**Data-Driven Marketing: The 15 Metrics
Everyone In Marketing Should Know**
by Mark Jeffrey

How to use simple, non-technical language to master
the latest analytic techniques to maximize marketing
Return On Investment.

INTERNET INSIGHTS

If you're going to do it, then do it right.

— John Baumberger, my father

Well, Dad, I couldn't agree more. Unfortunately, books are static and learning is dynamic so doing it right means continuously learning. To help you stay sharp, I've added a number of tools and additional materials that are free and instantly downloadable. I will add to these tools and materials as I uncover new insights and tips.

I'm offering these to you because being an innovator is hard. And everyone needs a helping hand.

You can find these materials on my website: msq.co

Here's a sample of what you'll find:

Free Innovation Framework
This framework is the foundation to take your fuzzy idea to firm reality. You can use it on your own, or with help from my team at *Marketsquare Worldwide* and *Duke University Innovation & Entrepeneurship*.

Free Map Templates
All of the map templates in this book are downloadable as full-page templates or graphic images.

Free FAQs
Many innovation challenges are similar. These Frequently Asked Questions will help you get up to speed and can be used to share how the IN-90 regimen will benefit your organization.

msq.co

INNOVATION CHANGES LIVES

EMILY K CENTER
BUILDING SCHOLARS – CHANGING LIVES

Proceeds from this book will go to support The Emily K Center in Durham, NC. The Center was established in 2006 with a mission to inspire academically-focused, low-income students to dream big, act with character and purpose, and reach their potential as leaders in their community.

The Center is named in honor of Emily Krzyzewski, a Polish immigrant who raised her family in a poor, racially diverse neighborhood on Chicago's North Side. Emily's husband, Bill, was an elevator operator, and Emily scrubbed floors and cleaned hotel rooms to provide support for her two children.

Emily's devotion and love, coupled with her amazing work ethic, provided her sons with an example they would follow the rest of their lives. Her eldest son, Bill, became a Captain in the Chicago Fire Department. Her younger son, Mike, became the winningest coach in the history of college basketball.

Emily also taught her sons to take advantage of opportunities wherever they presented themselves. Bill and Mike were fixtures at their local neighborhood community center. The community center offered young people and their families a chance to hone skills, make friends, and strengthen neighborhood ties—all key components to successful individuals and successful communities.

Today, the Emily K Center works diligently to match and surpass the opportunities that the Krzyzewski family found in Chicago. The Center's educational vehicle, the K to College Model, is designed to help students achieve in school, gain entry to college, and become the first in their families to earn a college degree.

These students are trying and transform their entire lives. The least you can do is transform your thinking about innovation!

Graduates from the Emily K Center proudly display their university choices.

ABOUT THE AUTHOR

Kurt Baumberger is the Managing Partner of the innovation consultancy MarketSquare Worldwide (msq.co), and an Innovation Fellow at Duke University. He works with companies and teams around the world.

Kurt is an entrepreneur, speaker, and author. He regularly speaks at business and innovation conferences. He also delivers workshops and programs to private clients.

He has always been an "idea man," starting his career as one of those "Mad Men" on Madison Avenue. Then, he worked at the world's premier international marketer, The Coca-Cola Company. This experience led to engagements with Apple, Microsoft, Nissan and other organizations that grow through innovation.

Kurt's first book, *Adapt Or Die: How The Internet Is Killing Dealer Profits And What To Do About It* helped the automotive industry innovate their business processes and even their entire business model. This book foresaw the impending automotive industry recession and provided detailed plans on how to survive and thrive on the rebound. It remains a "must read" for everyone in the industry today.

He graduated from the College of William and Mary with Honors in Social Psychology and earned his Masters of Business Administration at Duke University's Fuqua School of Business. While at Duke, he became friends with Coach Mike Krzyzewski and has been obsessed with Duke Basketball ever since.

In his spare time, he's played one-on-one with Michael Jordan, performed on stage with Jackson Browne, and has played golf with Jack Nicklaus. Each of these incredibly lucky experiences has a great story behind it.

Kurt grew up in a rural community in upstate New York and has lived in the thriving metropolises of New York City, Chicago, San Francisco, and Atlanta.

LET'S GO BUILD SOMETHING!

Need help building your team, finding fresh ideas,
getting customer feedback, or overcoming
organizational objections?

Contact Kurt Baumberger

kurt@msq.co

Need help with prototypes or digital proof of concepts
or enhancing your customer experience?

Contact Tom Fee

tom@msq.co

Need help with branding, design, or marketing to
launch your product or service innovation?

Contact Annika Kappenstein

anni@msq.co